Economies in Transition

An OED Evaluation of World Bank Assistance

http://www.worldbank.org/oed

2004
The World Bank
Washington, D.C.

Cover photo by Yuri Kozyrev, courtesy of the World Bank Photo Library.

ISBN 0-8213-5934-7
e-ISBN 0-8213-5935-5

Library of Congress Cataloging-in-Publication Data.

Galenson, Alice, 1948–
    Economies in transition : an OED evaluation of World Bank assistance / Alice C. Galenson.
        p. cm. — (Operations evaluation studies)
    Includes bibliographical references.
    ISBN 0-8213-5934-7
        1. Economic assistance—Europe. 2. Economic assistance—Asia. 3. World Bank. I. World Bank, Operations
Evaluation Dept. II. Title. III. World Bank operations evaluation study.

    HC240.G235 2004
    332.1'532–dc22

                                                            2004053252

World Bank InfoShop   Operations Evaluation Department
E-mail: pic@worldbank.org   Partnerships & Knowledge Programs (OEDPK)
Telephone: 202-458-5454   E-mail: eline@worldbank.org
Facsimilie: 202-522-1500   Telephone: 202-458-4497
                                                 Facsimilie: 202-522-3125

 Printed on Recycled Paper

Contents

Figures

Preface

This evaluation examines the Bank's assistance to the transition economies of the Europe and Central Asia Region since 1989. It is largely a meta-evaluation of Bank products and services in the transition countries, based on existing evaluative material—Country Assistance Evaluations (CAEs), Project Performance Assessment Reports (PPARs), Project and Implementation Completion Reports (PCRs, ICRs), Quality Assurance Group (QAG) data and reports, OED sectoral and thematic studies, and Bank-executed client surveys—as well as on other Bank strategic and project documents, economic and sector work, interviews, and literature from outside of the Bank. IFC and MIGA contributed information on their programs in the transition countries.

A series of background reports was commissioned for this study; they are noted in the Bibliography. A review of the literature captures the range of views on the Bank's role in supporting the transition, including alternative perspectives on methods of privatization. A Working Paper assesses the policies followed by the transition countries and the extent to which known alternatives might have resulted in superior outcomes. Another Working Paper reviews privatization and enterprise reform from the point of view of a Bank insider, elucidating the states of mind that prevailed in selected countries, the perceptions of the Bank at various times, the initial conditions faced by reformers and those who assisted them, and the policy frameworks that evolved. To complement the country-level evaluative material in CAEs and PPARs, and to learn more about Bank assistance from the point of view of the borrowers, papers were commissioned from former government officials and researchers in Hungary, Kazakhstan, and Poland; additional country views were found in Bank client surveys and in comments submitted by borrowers on CAEs and PPARs. Finally, five papers cover selected themes in depth: each one analyzes a particular area of Bank assistance to determine its expected contribution to the objectives of transition, the instruments used, and the relative success of these instruments in achieving the objectives.

An entry workshop was held in Washington on May 15, 2002. Speakers included experts from Hungary, Kazakhstan, Poland, and Russia; country and sectoral specialists from inside and outside the Bank; executive directors of the Bank representing transition countries; and Bank and IMF staff. A transcript of the workshop is available on OED's Web site.

This evaluation was financed in part by a grant from the Swiss Agency for Development and Cooperation (SDC) under the Bank-SDC Partnership Program on Development Effectiveness through Evaluation.

Acknowledgments

The task manager for this report was Alice Galenson. Thematic background papers were prepared by Robin Bates (energy), Raj Desai (private sector development), Pierre Landell-Mills (governance and public sector management), Fred Levy (financial sector), and Lawrence Thompson (social protection). Additional papers were written by Bruce Kogut and Andrew Spicer (review of the literature), John Nellis (the World Bank's role in privatization and enterprise reform), and Jan Svejnar (alternative policies). Views from borrowers were prepared by Gusztáv Báger (Hungary); Barbara Blaszczyk, Jacek Cukrowski, and Joanna Siwiñska (Poland); and Oraz Jandosov (Kazakhstan).

Two internal peer reviewers—Christopher Gerrard and Roberto Rocha—and four external peer reviewers—Marek Dabrowski (Deputy Chairman, Center for Social and Economic Research, Warsaw, Poland), Peter Murrell (Professor of Economics and Chair of the Academic Council of the Center for Institutional Reform and the Informal Sector, University of Maryland), Vanessa Mitchell-Thompson (Principal Econo-mist, EBRD), and Ivan Szegvari (Senior Economist, EBRD)—contributed detailed and valuable comments on the background papers and the final report. The study also benefited from the advice and support of Ruben Lamdany, former manager of the Country Evaluation and Regional Relations group of OED, and from many staff members of OED.

The financial support of the Swiss Agency for Development and Cooperation, along with their constructive comments on the background papers, is gratefully acknowledged.

OED received comments on an earlier draft of the report and on the background papers from the Bank's Europe and Central Asia (ECA) Regional management and from a number of current and former Bank staff involved in the Bank's assistance program to the transition countries.

Olga Vybornaia, Anar Omarova, Danuta Danilova, and Gulmira Karaguishiyeva provided statistical and research assistance; and Silvana Valle and Janice Joshi, administrative support. Caroline McEuen edited the report for publication.

Director-General, Operations Evaluation:
Gregory K. Ingram
Director, Operations Evaluation Department:
Ajay Chhibber
Senior Manager, Country Evaluation and
Regional Relations: *R. Kyle Peters*
Task Manager: *Alice Galenson*

FOREWORD

Much of Europe and Central Asia faced unprecedented political, economic, and social change after the break-up of the Soviet Union. The challenges to the transition were formidable, including deep economic distortions, major trade disruptions, and the absence of market-oriented institutions. As was foreseen, GDP fell sharply at the beginning of the period. In the Central and Eastern European countries, the transition recession was relatively shallow, but in the CIS (Commonwealth of Independent States), GDP fell an average of over 40 percent, and poverty and inequality increased sharply. No CIS country has yet regained its pre-transition per capita GDP.

The World Bank, in collaboration with the IMF, the European Union (EU), and other donors, geared up rapidly to support macroeconomic stabilization and structural reform. Many transition countries quickly accomplished price and trade liberalization. Small-scale privatization is virtually complete, and large-scale privatization is under way in most countries. While progress has been slower in financial sector reform, public sector reform, social protection, enterprise restructuring, and competition policy, the trend is upward. The private sector share of GDP across the transition countries is nearly 70 percent, and eight Central and Eastern European and Baltic countries have joined the EU. Much has been achieved, but much remains to be completed, especially in the CIS countries.

PRÓLOGO

Tras la división de la Unión Soviética, gran parte de Europa y Asia central experimentó cambios políticos, económicos y sociales sin precedentes. Esa transición planteó enormes desafíos, entre ellos profundos trastornos económicos, graves distorsiones del comercio y la falta de instituciones orientadas al mercado. Como se había pronosticado, el PIB sufrió una brusca caída al comienzo del período. En los países de Europa central y oriental, la recesión vinculada a la transición fue relativamente moderada, pero en la CEI (Comunidad de Estados Independientes), el PIB disminuyó en promedio más del 40%, y se registró un marcado aumento de la pobreza y la desigualdad. Ninguno de los países miembros de la CEI ha recuperado aún su PIB per cápita anterior a la transición.

El Banco Mundial, en colaboración con el FMI, la Unión Europea (UE) y otros donantes, se prepararon rápidamente para respaldar la estabilización macroeconómica y la reforma estructural. Muchos países en transición lograron liberalizar los precios y el comercio en poco tiempo. Las privatizaciones en pequeña escala ya han prácticamente terminado, y en la mayoría de los países está en marcha un proceso de privatizaciones en gran escala. Si bien los progresos en lo que respecta a la reforma del sector financiero, la reforma del sector público, los sistemas de protección social, la reestructuración de las empresas y la política de competencia han sido lentos, se observa una

AVANT-PROPOS

Une grande partie de l'Europe et de l'Asie centrale a été le théâtre de transformations politiques, économiques et sociales sans précédent après l'éclatement de l'Union soviétique. Les obstacles à surmonter au cours de cette transition étaient considérables : graves distorsions économiques, perturbations majeures au plan commercial et absence totale d'institutions favorisant les mécanismes du marché. Comme prévu, le PIB a brusquement chuté au début de cette période. Dans les pays d'Europe centrale et orientale, *les effets récessifs de la transition* ont été plutôt superficiels, mais dans le Commonwealth des États indépendants (CEI), le PIB a baissé de plus de 40 % en moyenne, et la pauvreté et les inégalités se sont nettement accrues. Dans aucun pays du CEI, le PIB par habitant n'a encore retrouvé le niveau d'avant la transition.

La Banque mondiale, en collaboration avec le Fonds monétaire international (FMI), l'Union européenne (UE) et d'autres bailleurs de fonds, s'est rapidement préparée à contribuer à la stabilisation économique et aux réformes structurelles. De nombreux pays en transition ont rapidement libéralisé les prix et le commerce. La privatisation des petites entreprises touche à sa fin et la plupart des pays ont entrepris de privatiser leurs grandes entreprises. Dans d'autres domaines, comme le secteur financier, le secteur public, la protection sociale, la restructuration des entreprises et la politique de la concurrence, les progrès sont moins rapides, mais l'évo-

ENGLISH

In assessing the effectiveness of Bank assistance, it must be recognized that the collapse of the Soviet Union and the ensuing transition took place with little warning and on an unparalleled scale. Political pressures compelled the Bank to move quickly and lend large amounts. Staff were frequently confronted with the need to act, often under difficult circumstances, in the absence of relevant experience or country knowledge, learning along the way.

Overall, Bank assistance to the transition countries has been successful, but there were mistakes early on when the true nature of transition was not fully understood. Not unexpectedly, the Bank's evolving knowledge and the rapidly changing circumstances led to many mid-course corrections. The strategy was to promote macroeconomic stability and sound economic management; reorient and strengthen public sector institutions; build the basic institutions of a market economy and an enabling environment for private sector initiatives; and cushion the social cost of the transition. These objectives were relevant, but effectiveness was limited by an initial underestimation of the need to focus on poverty alleviation and good governance and the use of rapid privatization to promote private sector development (PSD) without a supporting legal and institutional framework. Lending was based on the expectation of a short, shallow transition recession; the prolonged recession in some CIS countries led to the accumulation of significant levels of indebtedness. The Bank internalized emerging lessons and shifted its emphasis ac-

ESPAÑOL

tendencia ascendente. En todos los países en transición, la cuota del PIB correspondiente al sector privado es de casi 70%, y los ocho países de Europa central y oriental y del Báltico están listos para incorporarse a la UE. Es mucho lo que se ha logrado, pero aún queda una larga lista de cuestiones pendientes, sobre todo en los países de la CEI.

Al evaluar la eficacia de la asistencia prestada por el Banco Mundial, es preciso reconocer que el colapso de la Unión Soviética y la transición subsiguiente se produjeron en forma bastante sorpresiva y a una escala sin parangón. Las presiones políticas obligaron al Banco a actuar con rapidez y prestar grandes cantidades de dinero. El personal se vio muchas veces en la necesidad de actuar, a menudo en circunstancias difíciles, sin la debida experiencia o el conocimiento suficiente del país, por lo que debió aprender sobre la marcha.

En términos generales, la asistencia prestada por el Banco a los países con economías en transición ha sido satisfactoria, pero se cometieron errores al principio, cuando no se tenía una comprensión cabal de la verdadera índole de la transición. Como era de esperar, a medida que evolucionaban los conocimientos del Banco y las circunstancias cambiaban rápidamente, fue necesario introducir muchas correcciones sobre la marcha. La estrategia consistió en promover la estabilidad macroeconómica y una gestión económica racional; reorientar y fortalecer las instituciones del sector público; crear las instituciones básicas de una economía de mercado y un entorno propicio para las iniciativas del sector privado, y amortiguar los efectos del costo

FRANÇAIS

lution actuelle laisse bien présager de l'avenir. La part du secteur privé dans le PIB de l'ensemble des pays en transition est de 70 %, et huit pays baltes et d'Europe centrale et orientale sont sur le point d'entrer dans l'UE. Des progrès importants ont été réalisés, mais il reste beaucoup à faire, surtout dans les pays du CEI.

Pour évaluer l'efficacité de l'aide de la Banque, il ne faut pas perdre de vue que l'effondrement de l'Union soviétique et la transition qui s'en est suivie sont intervenus sans beaucoup de préavis et ont eu une ampleur sans précédent. Sous la pression d'impératifs politiques, la Banque a dû agir vite et prêter des sommes importantes. Ses services ont fréquemment été contraints d'intervenir dans des conditions souvent difficiles, apprenant sur le tas, sans avoir acquis l'expérience ni la connaissance nécessaires des pays.

Globalement l'aide de la Banque aux pays en transition est concluante même si des erreurs ont été commises initialement lorsque la véritable nature de la transition n'était pas encore parfaitement connue. On ne peut donc s'étonner que les connaissances accumulées par la Banque et l'évolution rapide de la situation aient conduit à rectifier le cap à plusieurs reprises au fil du temps. La stratégie a été d'encourager la stabilité macroéconomique, favoriser une gestion économique solide, réorienter et renforcer les institutions du secteur public, mettre en place les rouages essentiels d'une économie de marché, créer un environnement favorable au secteur privé et amortir le coût social de la transition. Ces objectifs étaient bons, mais deux facteurs ont limité l'effi-

ENGLISH

cordingly: poverty monitoring and alleviation and good governance are now prominent objectives in both lending and analytical work, and the approach to privatization and PSD has evolved considerably.

The following recommendations emerged from a detailed study of PSD, governance, public sector management (PSM) and institution building, the financial sector, social protection, and energy in the transition economies:

- Legal and judicial reform, with an emphasis on implementation, is critical for improvements in the business climate, the financial sector, social protection, and governance in general.
- Financial sector lending should be conditioned on progress in enforcing prudential regulations and international accounting standards, and raising the effectiveness of bank supervision. Training of bank supervisors, judges, auditors, and other skilled professionals needed to make the system work should be a priority.
- In the energy sector improved commercial performance and corporate governance are priorities. The sequencing of reforms, including the feasibility of immediate privatization, depends on country circumstances.
- Privatization of large enterprises should focus on encouraging a carefully prepared, transparent, competitive process, open to foreign participation.
- A strategic approach, distinguished by the capacity of the country, is needed for pension reform and for better targeting of

ESPAÑOL

social de la transición. Estos objetivos eran acertados, pero la eficacia se vio limitada por una subestimación inicial de la necesidad de centrar la atención en el alivio de la pobreza y una buena gestión de gobierno, y por el recurso a las privatizaciones rápidas para fomentar el desarrollo del sector privado sin un marco jurídico e institucional que lo sustentara. El financiamiento se basó en la creencia de que la recesión vinculada a la transición sería corta y moderada; la prolongada recesión en algunos países de la CEI dio lugar a la acumulación de altos niveles de endeudamiento. El Banco internalizó las nuevas enseñanzas recogidas y cambió su enfoque para adecuarlo a ellas: la vigilancia y el alivio de la pobreza y la buena gestión de gobierno son actualmente objetivos primordiales tanto de la concesión de préstamos como de la labor analítica, y la forma de encarar las privatizaciones y el desarrollo del sector privado ha evolucionado considerablemente.

Las recomendaciones siguientes surgieron de un estudio detallado del desarrollo del sector privado, la gestión de gobierno, la administración del sector público y el fortalecimiento institucional, el sector financiero, los sistemas de protección social y la energía en los países con economías en transición:

- La reforma legal y judicial, centrada en el cumplimiento, son fundamentales para mejorar el clima comercial, el sector financiero, los sistemas de protección social y la gestión de gobierno en general.
- Los préstamos al sector financiero deberían condicionarse a los progresos en la aplicación de regla-

FRANÇAIS

cacité de la stratégie : la nécessité de privilégier systématiquement la lutte contre la pauvreté et la bonne gouvernance a été sous-estimée, et, en l'absence d'un cadre légal et institutionnel propice, l'effort de développement du secteur privé par la privatisation rapide des entreprises n'a pas toujours porté les fruits attendus. Le volume de prêt reposait sur l'hypothèse d'une récession superficielle et éphémère liée à la transition. Dans certains pays du CEI, la longue récession a conduit à un niveau d'endettement élevé. La Banque a internalisé les enseignements se dégageant de ses interventions et a recentré son action en conséquence. Le suivi et la réduction de la pauvreté, tout comme la bonne gouvernance, sont aujourd'hui au cœur des opérations de prêt et du travail d'analyse, et la façon d'aborder la privatisation et le développement du secteur privé a considérablement évolué.

Les recommandations suivantes sont le fruit d'une étude détaillée du développement du secteur privé ; de la gouvernance, de la gestion du secteur privé et du renforcement des institutions ; du secteur financier ; de la protection sociale ; et de l'énergie dans les pays en transition.

- La réforme du système juridique et judiciaire est d'une importance critique pour améliorer le climat des affaires, le secteur financier, la protection sociale et la gouvernance en général. L'accent doit être placé sur l'application de la législation.
- Dans le secteur financier, l'octroi de prêts devrait être subordonné à la réalisation de progrès dans

other social assistance programs.

The study presents a number of findings that cut across sectors and lend themselves to recommendations that are broadly applicable, not only to the transition countries, but to many others as well:

- When the Bank begins to work in a country—or after a long hiatus—lending should be held to prudent levels until a solid knowledge base is established, with convincing evidence of government and societal ownership of the programs.
- The rate of progress of any reform is largely determined by government ownership, and a well-informed civil society can become a major driver for change. Country assistance strategies should promote ownership and consensus for reform through capacity building for governments and civil society and through analysis of the political, social, and economic processes that affect stakeholder behavior. Recent Bank initiatives promoting stakeholder awareness and participation in several countries bear wider replication.
- A comprehensive, long-term approach is needed in developing strategies for institutional change and PSM reform. Analytical work on governance and PSM should precede large amounts of Bank lending, particularly where problems are likely to affect assistance programs.
- Economic and sector work can serve to increase knowledge and train researchers; its quality in the transition countries has been high,

mentaciones prudentes y normas internacionales de contabilidad y a una supervisión más eficaz del sistema bancario. Debería asignarse prioridad a la capacitación de supervisores de los bancos, jueces, auditores y otros profesionales idóneos necesarios para que el sistema funcione.

- En el sector de la energía es prioritario mejorar el desempeño comercial y el gobierno de las empresas. El orden en que deben introducirse las reformas, así como la factibilidad de la privatización inmediata, dependen de las circunstancias de cada país.
- La privatización de las grandes empresas debería hacer hincapié en alentar un proceso de licitación cuidadosamente preparado, transparente y competitivo, abierto a la participación extranjera.
- Es necesario adoptar un enfoque estratégico que distinga según la capacidad de cada país, para la reforma del sistema de pensiones y para mejorar la orientación de otros programas de asistencia social.

El estudio expone una serie de conclusiones pertinentes a varios sectores y que permiten formular recomendaciones aplicables en un plano más amplio, no solamente a los países en transición sino también a muchos otros:

- Cuando el Banco comienza a trabajar en un país —o después de un largo período de inactividad—, el monto de los préstamos debería mantenerse dentro de límites prudentes, hasta que se haya establecido una base de conocimientos sólidos, con pruebas convincentes de que el gobierno

l'application des réglementations prudentielles et des normes comptables internationales ainsi qu'à une plus grande efficacité du contrôle bancaire. La formation des personnes chargées d'exercer un contrôle bancaire, des juges, des auditeurs et des autres professionnels nécessaires dans ce secteur doit être une priorité.

- Dans le secteur de l'énergie, l'amélioration des résultats commerciaux et du gouvernement d'entreprise sont des priorités. L'ordre dans lequel doivent se faire les réformes, notamment la faisabilité d'une privatisation immédiate, dépend des conditions particulières de chaque pays.
- La privatisation des grandes entreprises doit s'articuler sur un mécanisme soigneusement préparé, transparent et ouvert à la concurrence, y compris étrangère.
- Il faut arrêter une stratégie claire, adaptée aux capacités propres à chaque pays, pour réformer le régime des retraites et pour améliorer le ciblage des autres programmes d'aide sociale.

La présente étude débouche sur plusieurs conclusions recoupant divers domaines d'intervention et conduisant à des recommandations applicables de façon très générale non seulement aux pays en transition mais également à bien d'autres pays.

- Lorsque la Banque entame pour la première fois des activités dans un pays — ou lorsqu'elle y reprend ses activités après une longue interruption —, la plus grande prudence est de rigueur

ENGLISH

but its impact on the country dialogue might have been greater had it been more relevant and timely.
- Greater transparency can increase public accountability and discourage corruption. The Bank needs to implement fully its own disclosure policies and disseminate its analytical work, and encourage governments to report more regularly and fully to both their parliaments and the public.
- The Bank can be better prepared to identify and address rapidly growing poverty by giving high priority to the monitoring of poverty levels from the beginning of its involvement in a country.
- Aid coordination can increase the effectiveness of all assistance. Recipient governments should lead aid coordination, with donors helping them define clear development strategies, including monitorable action plans for implementation.

ESPAÑOL

y la sociedad se identifican con los programas.
- El grado de progreso de cualquier reforma depende en gran parte de que el gobierno sienta esa reforma como propia, y una sociedad civil bien informada puede convertirse en una importante fuerza impulsora del cambio. Las estrategias de asistencia a los países deberían promover el sentido de identificación y el consenso en torno a las reformas, mediante el fortalecimiento de la capacidad de los gobiernos y de la sociedad civil y el análisis de los procesos políticos, sociales y económicos que afectan el comportamiento de las partes interesadas. Las iniciativas recientes del Banco que promueven la sensibilización y la participación de las partes interesadas en varios países merecen ser aplicadas en forma más generalizada.
- La elaboración de estrategias para el cambio institucional y la reforma de la administración del sector público deben encararse con un criterio amplio y a largo plazo. El Banco debe hacer un análisis de la gestión de gobierno y la administración del sector público antes de otorgar préstamos, en particular cuando existe la probabilidad de que los problemas afecten los programas de asistencia.
- Las actividades económicas y sectoriales pueden servir para ampliar los conocimientos y capacitar investigadores; su calidad en los países en transición ha sido alta, pero su influencia en el diálogo nacional podría haber sido mayor si hubiera sido más pertinente y oportuna.
- Una mayor transparencia puede mejorar la rendición de cuentas en

FRANÇAIS

dans l'octroi des prêts aussi longtemps que l'on ne dispose pas de connaissances solides ni d'éléments permettant d'établir clairement que les pouvoirs publics et la société reprennent les actions menées à leur propre compte.
- Le rythme de progression des réformes dépend pour beaucoup de l'adhésion des pouvoirs publics, et une société civile bien informé, peut devenir un puissant facteur de changement. Les stratégies d'aide-pays doivent favoriser l'appropriation des réformes et l'émergence d'un consensus, par le biais d'un renforcement des capacités des pouvoirs publics et de la société civile et d'une analyse des processus politiques, sociaux et économiques ayant une incidence sur le comportement des parties prenantes. Les récentes initiatives de la Banque ayant pour objet de susciter une prise de conscience de la part des parties prenantes et d'encourager leur participation dans plusieurs pays devraient être largement reproduites.
- La transformation des institutions et la réforme de la gestion du secteur public doit s'inscrire dans une stratégie globale à long terme. Un travail analytique sur la gouvernance et la gestion du secteur public doit être effectué avant que la Banque ne décide d'octroyer des prêts importants, surtout lorsque des problèmes risquent de porter atteinte aux programmes d'aide.
- Le travail économique et sectoriel peut servir à renforcer les connaissances et à former des chercheurs. Il a été de qualité

ESPAÑOL

el sector público y desalentar la corrupción. El Banco debe aplicar plenamente sus propias políticas de libre acceso a la información y difundir su labor analítica, como así también alentar a los gobiernos a presentar informes más completos y periódicos a sus parlamentos y al público.

- El Banco puede estar mejor preparado para detectar rápidamente un aumento de la pobreza y tomar medidas paliativas si asigna mayor prioridad al seguimiento de los niveles de pobreza desde el comienzo de su actuación en un país.

- La coordinación de la ayuda puede aumentar la eficacia de toda la asistencia. Los gobiernos receptores deberían dirigir la coordinación de la ayuda, con la colaboración de los donantes en cuanto a definir estrategias claras de desarrollo, incluidos planes de acción para la aplicación susceptibles de seguimiento.

FRANÇAIS

dans les pays en transition, mais son impact sur le dialogue avec les pays aurait pu être plus important s'il avait été plus pertinent et s'il était venu plus à son heure.

- Une plus grande transparence peut aider à responsabiliser le secteur public et à prévenir la corruption. La Banque doit appliquer systématiquement sa propre politique de diffusion de l'information et faire connaître son travail d'analyse. Elle doit aussi encourager les autorités à faire rapport de façon plus régulière et plus complète au corps législatif et à la population.

- La Banque sera mieux à même d'identifier et de combattre la montée rapide de la pauvreté si elle s'attache davantage à en surveiller les niveaux dès le commencement de ses activités dans un pays.

- La coordination de l'aide peut contribuer à renforcer l'efficacité de tout le dispositif d'aide. Les gouvernements bénéficiaires doivent piloter la coordination de l'aide, les bailleurs de fonds se chargeant de les aider à définir des stratégies de développement claires et notamment des plans d'action vérifiables.

Gregory K. Ingram
Director-General, Operations Evaluation

ENGLISH

EXECUTIVE SUMMARY

Large parts of Europe and Central Asia (ECA) have undergone unprecedented political, economic, and social change since 1989, when the Soviet Union began to break up—a change often referred to as the *transition*. The challenges to this transition were formidable, including deep economic distortions, major trade disruptions, and a total lack of market-oriented institutions. As was foreseen, gross domestic product (GDP) fell sharply at the beginning of the period. In the Central and Eastern European countries, the *transition recession* was relatively shallow and short-lived; GDP fell on average by less than 15 percent, and per capita incomes recovered in many countries before the end of the decade. However, in the former Soviet Union (hereafter referred to as the Commonwealth of Independent States, CIS), the decline was far more severe than expected. GDP fell on average by over 40 percent, and although growth has picked up strongly in recent years, no CIS country has yet regained its pre-transition per capita GDP. Poverty increased well beyond expectations in many CIS countries, and inequality rose as well. Infant mortality fell in most of the transition countries, but life expectancy fell as well in most CIS countries. The gross enrollment rate in basic education fell in many of the transition countries.

The World Bank, in collaboration with the International Monetary Fund (IMF), the European Union (EU), and other donors, geared up rapidly to support macroeconomic

ESPAÑOL

RESUMEN

En gran parte de Europa y Asia central se han producido cambios políticos, económicos y sociales sin precedentes desde 1989, cuando comenzó a dividirse la Unión Soviética, cambio que con frecuencia se denomina la *transición*. Esa transición planteó enormes desafíos, entre ellos profundos trastornos económicos, graves distorsiones del comercio y la falta de instituciones orientadas al mercado. Como se había pronosticado, el producto interno bruto (PIB) sufrió una brusca caída al comienzo del período. En los países de Europa central y oriental, la *recesión vinculada a la transición* fue relativamente moderada y de corta duración; el PIB disminuyó menos del 15% como promedio, y el ingreso per cápita se recuperó en muchos países antes del final del decenio. Sin embargo, en la ex Unión Soviética (en lo sucesivo denominada Comunidad de Estados Independientes (CEI)), la declinación fue mucho más grave de lo que se esperaba. El PIB se redujo en promedio más del 40%, y si bien el crecimiento ha vuelto a adquirir un fuerte impulso ascendente en los últimos años, ninguno de los países miembros de la CEI ha recuperado aún su PIB per cápita anterior a la transición. En muchos países de la CEI, la pobreza aumentó mucho más de lo que se preveía, y lo mismo ocurrió con la desigualdad. La mortalidad infantil disminuyó en la mayoría de los países en transición, pero la esperanza de vida también se redujo en la mayoría de los países de la CEI. La tasa bruta de matrícula en la enseñanza básica dismi-

FRANÇAIS

RÉSUMÉ ANALYTIQUE

Depuis 1989, début de l'éclatement de l'Union soviétique, une grande partie de la région Europe et Asie centrale (ECA), est le théâtre de transformations politiques, économiques et sociales sans précédent, souvent regroupées sous le vocable *transition*. Les obstacles à surmonter étaient considérables : graves distorsions économiques, perturbations majeures au plan commercial et absence totale d'institutions favorisant les mécanismes du marché. Comme prévu, le produit intérieur brut (PIB) a brusquement chuté au début de cette période. Dans les pays d'Europe centrale et orientale (PECO), *les effets récessifs de la transition* ont été plutôt superficiels et éphémères. En moyenne, le PIB a reculé de moins de 15 % et, dans de nombreux pays, le revenu par habitant s'était redressé à la fin de la décennie. En revanche, dans l'ex-Union soviétique (le Commonwealth des États indépendants, le CEI, comme on le désignera ici), le repli a été beaucoup plus marqué que prévu. Le PIB a baissé de plus de 40 % en moyenne et, malgré la reprise de ces dernières années, aucun pays de la CEI n'a encore retrouvé le niveau d'avant la transition. Dans beaucoup de ces pays, la pauvreté s'est accrue nettement plus que prévu et les inégalités se sont creusées. La mortalité infantile a baissé dans la majorité des pays en transition, mais l'espérance de vie a aussi reculé dans la plupart des pays de la CEI. Le taux brut de scolarisation dans l'éducation de base est également tombé dans beaucoup de pays en transition.

ENGLISH

stabilization and structural reform (and later, in South-eastern Europe—SEE—to provide post-conflict support). In most countries, policy reform has progressed steadily, with few reversals. Within the first few years, many transition countries had undertaken comprehensive price and trade liberalization, and quite a few had achieved substantial privatization of small enterprises. At present, small-scale privatization is virtually complete, and large-scale privatization is under way in most countries. While progress has been slower in financial sector reform, public sector reform, social protection, enterprise restructuring, and competition policy, the trend is still upward, with reforms either being planned or under implementation. Substantial overall progress has been achieved: the private sector share of GDP across all transition countries reached nearly 70 percent in 2002 from virtually nil in 1989, even including the late-starting post-conflict SEE countries and the most reluctant reformers. Eight Central and Eastern Europe and Baltic (CEB) countries joined the EU this year, and two others are expected to join in the next several years.

In assessing the effectiveness of Bank assistance, it must be recognized that the collapse of the Soviet Union and the ensuing transition took place with little warning and on an unparalleled scale. Political imperatives put the Bank under pressure to move quickly and lend large amounts, and staff were frequently confronted with the need to act, often under difficult circumstances, in the absence of relevant experience and with virtually no country

ESPAÑOL

nuyó en muchos de los países en transición.

El Banco Mundial, en colaboración con el Fondo Monetario Internacional (FMI), la Unión Europea (UE) y otros donantes, se preparó rápidamente para respaldar la estabilización macroeconómica y la reforma estructural (y luego en Europa sudoriental, para prestar apoyo en el período posterior al conflicto). En la mayoría de los países, la reforma de las políticas ha avanzado a pasos firmes, con pocas contramarchas. En los primeros años de la transición, muchos países liberaron completamente los precios y el comercio, y varios países lograron privatizar un gran número de pequeñas empresas. En el momento actual, las privatizaciones en pequeña escala ya han prácticamente terminado, y en la mayoría de los países está en marcha un proceso de privatizaciones en gran escala. Si bien los progresos en lo que respecta a la reforma del sector financiero, la reforma del sector público, los sistemas de protección social, la reestructuración de las empresas y la política de competencia han sido lentos, la tendencia sigue siendo ascendente, con reformas en etapa de planificación o ejecución. En términos generales, los progresos han sido considerables: en todos los países en transición, la participación del sector privado en el PIB llegó a ser de casi 70% en 2002 a partir de prácticamente cero en 1989, incluso en los países de Europa sudoriental que se sumaron tardíamente a la transición en la etapa posterior al conflicto y en los países más renuentes a las reformas. Ocho países de Europa central y oriental y del Báltico se incorporaron a la Unión Europea este año, y se prevé la incorporación de

FRANÇAIS

La Banque mondiale, en collaboration avec le Fonds monétaire international (FMI), l'Union européenne (UE) et d'autres bailleurs de fonds, s'est rapidement préparée à contribuer à la stabilisation économique et aux réformes structurelles (puis à fournir une aide aux pays du Sud-Est sortant d'un conflit). Dans la plupart des pays, les réformes progressent rapidement et les revirements sont rares. Dès les premières années, beaucoup des pays s'étaient engagés sur la voie d'une vaste libéralisation des prix et du commerce, et un bon nombre d'entre eux avaient privatisé de multiples petites entreprises. Ce dernier aspect touche aujourd'hui à sa fin et la plupart des pays sont maintenant en train de privatiser les grandes entreprises. Dans d'autres domaines, comme le secteur financier, le secteur public, la protection sociale, la restructuration des entreprises et la politique de la concurrence, les progrès sont moins rapides, mais les réformes prévues ou en cours laissent bien présager de l'avenir. Globalement, des progrès importants ont été réalisés, la part du secteur privé dans le PIB de l'ensemble des pays en transition étant passée de quasiment 0 % en 1989 à près de 70 % en 2002, même si l'on tient compte des pays d'Europe du Sud-Est qui, sortis d'un conflit, ont démarré plus tard, et des pays qui étaient les plus réticents à entreprendre des réformes. Huit PECO et pays baltes sont entrés dans l'UE cette année, et deux autres devraient le faire dans les années qui viennent.

Pour évaluer l'efficacité de l'aide de la Banque, il ne faut pas perdre de vue que l'effondrement de l'Union soviétique et la transition qui s'en est

ENGLISH

knowledge, learning along the way. The Bank's role, though small relative to overall financial flows—except in a few small countries—was significant in terms of analytical work and policy advice. This report, a meta-evaluation largely based on previous evaluative work, and with the acknowledged benefit of 20/20 hindsight, attempts to identify the lessons to be learned from this extreme experience, in the hopes that they will prove useful in countries undergoing similar, if less extreme, changes in the future.

The Bank's assistance to the transition countries was on the whole successful, but clearly there were mistakes early on when the true nature of transition was not yet fully understood. Not unexpectedly, the Bank's evolving knowledge and the rapidly changing circumstances led to many course corrections along the way. Of the nine Country Assistance Evaluations (CAEs) undertaken by OED for transition countries, six rate the outcome of the country program satisfactory, at least for the most recent time period (Bulgaria, Kazakhstan, Kyrgyz Republic, Lithuania, Poland, and Russia). CAEs rated the outcome of the country programs in Albania, Azerbaijan, and Ukraine, as well as the earlier periods in Bulgaria and Russia, unsatisfactory.[1]

The Bank's strategy was to promote macroeconomic stability and sound economic management, reorient and strengthen public sector institutions, build the basic institutions of a market economy and an enabling environment for private sector initiatives, and cushion the social cost of the transition. These

ESPAÑOL

dos más en los próximos años.

Al evaluar la eficacia de la asistencia prestada por el Banco, es preciso reconocer que el colapso de la Unión Soviética y la transición subsiguiente se produjeron en forma bastante sorpresiva y a una escala sin parangón. Las urgencias políticas presionaron al Banco a actuar con rapidez y prestar grandes cantidades de dinero, y el personal se vio muchas veces en la necesidad de actuar, a menudo en circunstancias difíciles, sin la debida experiencia y con un desconocimiento prácticamente total de los países, por lo que debió aprender sobre la marcha. El papel que desempeñó el Banco, aunque reducido en comparación con el volumen total de flujos financieros —salvo en unos pocos países pequeños— fue muy importante en lo que respecta a la labor analítica y el asesoramiento en materia de políticas. El presente informe, que es una meta-evaluación basada principalmente en trabajos de evaluación anteriores, y cuenta con la reconocida ventaja que otorga una clara visión retrospectiva, trata de identificar las enseñanzas que ha dejado esta experiencia extrema, con la esperanza de que puedan resultar útiles en países que sufran cambios similares, aunque no tan extremos, en el futuro.

La asistencia prestada por el Banco a los países con economías en transición fue satisfactoria en términos generales, pero es indudable que se cometieron errores al principio, cuando no se tenía una comprensión cabal de la verdadera índole de la transición. Como era de esperar, a medida que evolucionaban los conocimientos del Banco y las circunstancias cambiaban rápidamente, fue

FRANÇAIS

suivie sont intervenus sans beaucoup de préavis et ont eu une ampleur sans précédent. Sous la pression d'impératifs politiques, la Banque a dû agir vite et prêter des sommes importantes. Ses services ont fréquemment été contraints d'intervenir dans des conditions souvent difficiles, apprenant sur le tas, sans avoir acquis l'expérience nécessaire ou avoir une connaissance suffisante des pays. Par son travail d'analyse et ses conseils sur les réformes, la Banque a joué un rôle important, bien que limité au regard du volume total de financement, sauf dans quelques pays. Métaévaluation reposant largement elle-même sur d'autres évaluations, et établi avec tout le bénéfice du recul nécessaire, ce rapport cherche à dégager des enseignements de cette expérience extrême dans l'espoir que les acquis serviront aux autres pays qui seront à l'avenir confrontés à des changements similaires, même s'ils sont moins radicaux.

Globalement l'aide de la Banque aux pays en transition a été concluante même si, de toute évidence, des erreurs ont été commises initialement lorsque la véritable nature de la transition n'était pas encore parfaitement connue. On ne peut donc s'étonner que les connaissances accumulées par la Banque et l'évolution rapide de la situation aient conduit à rectifier le cap à plusieurs reprises au fil du temps. Sur les neuf évaluations de l'aide aux pays en transition réalisées par l'OED, six ont jugé « satisfaisants » les résultats des programmes, au moins pour la période la plus récente (Bulgarie, Kazakhstan, Lituanie, Pologne, République kirghize et Russie). En revanche, ces programmes ont été

ENGLISH

objectives were relevant. The initial strategy's effectiveness, however, was limited for two reasons. First, it underestimated until the late 1990s the need to focus systematically on poverty alleviation and good governance. Second, the use of rapid privatization to promote private sector development did not always achieve its intended effect without a supporting legal and institutional framework. Over time, the Bank internalized emerging lessons and shifted its emphasis accordingly: poverty monitoring and alleviation and good governance are now prominent objectives in both lending and analytical work, and the approach to privatization and private sector development has evolved considerably.

A side effect of the prolonged transition recession in the CIS has been the build-up of significant debt problems in some countries that started with very little debt. Official lending levels were based on the expectation that the transition recession would be shallow and of short duration. In countries where the recession was far deeper and longer than foreseen, and problems of governance more serious than anticipated, this has resulted in significant levels of indebtedness. The effects of this debt are likely to be long lasting. In these countries, with the benefit of hindsight, more prudent lending levels would have been better for the long run.

It is increasingly evident that many countries in Europe and Central Asia no longer fit the standard *transition* model. For the CEB countries that are integrating into Western Europe, issues facing middle-income countries may be most relevant. Others fit

ESPAÑOL

necesario introducir muchas correcciones sobre la marcha. De las nueve evaluaciones de la asistencia prestada a los países en transición realizadas por el Departamento de Evaluación de Operaciones (DEO), seis consideran que los resultados del programa para el país fueron satisfactorios, por lo menos en el período más reciente. Según esta misma evaluación, los resultados del programa en Albania, Azerbaiyán y Ucrania, así como en los períodos iniciales en Bulgaria y Rusia, fueron insatisfactorios[1].

La estrategia del Banco consistió en promover la estabilidad macroeconómica y una gestión económica racional; reorientar y fortalecer las instituciones del sector público; crear las instituciones básicas de una economía de mercado y un entorno propicio para las iniciativas del sector privado, y amortiguar los efectos del costo social de la transición. Estos objetivos eran acertados. Sin embargo, la eficacia de la estrategia inicial se vio limitada por dos motivos. El primero es que, hasta fines del decenio de 1990, se subestimó la necesidad de prestar una atención sistemática al alivio de la pobreza y la buena gestión de gobierno. En segundo lugar, el recurso a las privatizaciones rápidas para fomentar el desarrollo del sector privado no siempre logró los efectos deseados, al no existir un marco jurídico e institucional que lo sustentara. Con el tiempo, el Banco internalizó las nuevas enseñanzas recogidas y cambió su enfoque para adecuarlo a ellas: la vigilancia y el alivio de la pobreza así como la buena gestión de gobierno son actualmente objetivos primordiales tanto de la concesión de préstamos como de la labor analítica, y la

FRANÇAIS

jugés « insatisfaisants » en Albanie, en Azerbaïdjan et en Ukraine, ainsi qu'en Bulgarie et en Russie pendant leur période initiale[1].

La stratégie de la Banque a été d'encourager la stabilité macroéconomique, favoriser une gestion économique solide, réorienter et renforcer les institutions du secteur public, mettre en place les rouages essentiels d'une économie de marché, créer un environnement favorable au secteur privé et amortir le coût social de la transition. Ces objectifs étaient bons. Deux facteurs ont toutefois limité initialement l'efficacité de la stratégie. D'une part, la nécessité de privilégier systématiquement la lutte contre la pauvreté et la bonne gouvernance a été sous-estimée. D'autre part, en l'absence d'un cadre légal et institutionnel propice, l'effort de développement du secteur privé par la privatisation rapide des entreprises n'a pas toujours porté les fruits attendus. Au fil du temps, la Banque a internalisé les enseignements se dégageant de ses interventions et a recentré son action en conséquence. Le suivi et la réduction de la pauvreté, tout comme la bonne gouvernance, sont aujourd'hui au cœur des opérations de prêt et du travail d'analyse, et la façon d'aborder la privatisation et le développement du secteur privé a considérablement évolué.

Les problèmes d'endettement apparus dans certains pays auparavant très peu endettés sont l'un des effets secondaires de la longue récession liée à la transition dans le CEI. Le niveau des prêts de sources publiques reposait sur l'hypothèse d'une récession superficielle et éphémère. Là où la récession a été

ENGLISH

more appropriately into categories such as highly indebted, post-conflict, or low-income countries under stress. The issues faced by Hungary and the Czech Republic are quite different from those of Turkmenistan and the Kyrgyz Republic. While the term *transition* was used to discuss their transformation to market-based economies, the label *transition economies* no longer seems as relevant. However, the lessons from this period—brought into sharper relief by the large scale of the transition—can be applied more generally.

This evaluation examines in depth five areas of Bank assistance, chosen for their importance to the Bank's lending program and their potential for yielding lessons that are useful for both the remaining transition agenda and more broadly: private sector development; governance, public sector management and institution building; the financial sector; social protection; and energy. It does not include an in-depth review of all areas where the Bank was active. The Bank's experience in price and trade liberalization, where significant achievements were realized and sustained, is not reviewed. Some areas have been covered in other OED evaluations, such as a review of agricultural policy reform, which found considerable advances in agricultural trade liberalization, land reform, and the development of rural financial markets, with less progress in postprivatization follow-up and the reform of state institutions. Other areas, such as trade, are covered by ongoing OED evaluations. The following sections summarize the findings and recommendations specific to the five areas covered by this evaluation. The final section presents some crosscutting

ESPAÑOL

forma de encarar las privatizaciones y el desarrollo del sector privado ha evolucionado considerablemente.

Un efecto colateral de la prolongada recesión vinculada a la transición en la CEI ha sido la acumulación de graves problemas de endeudamiento en algunos países que iniciaron la transición con una deuda muy pequeña. El monto de los préstamos oficiales otorgados se basó en la creencia de que la recesión vinculada a la transición sería moderada y de corta duración. En los países en que la recesión fue mucho más profunda y prolongada de lo previsto, el resultado han sido altos niveles de endeudamiento. Es probable que los efectos de esta deuda perduren por mucho tiempo. Si se analiza la situación en retrospectiva, en el largo plazo hubiera sido mejor para esos países que el volumen de los préstamos se hubiera limitado a montos más prudentes.

Es cada vez más evidente que muchos países de Europa y Asia central ya no encuadran en el modelo corriente de "transición". En el caso de los países de Europa central y oriental y del Báltico que se están integrando a Europa occidental, pueden ser más pertinentes las cuestiones que afectan a los países de ingreso mediano. Otros países encuadran mejor en categorías como las de países fuertemente endeudados, en situación de posguerra, o de ingreso bajo en dificultades. Los problemas que enfrentan Hungría y la República Checa son muy diferentes de los que aquejan a Turkmenistán y la República Kirguisa. Mientras que el término *transición* se utilizaba para hacer referencia a su transformación en economías basadas en el mer-

FRANÇAIS

beaucoup plus marquée et longue que prévue et les problèmes de gouvernance plus graves qu'envisagés, l'endettement atteint un niveau élevé. Cette dette risque d'avoir des effets durables. Avec le recul, des opérations de prêt plus limitées auraient été plus judicieuses à terme pour ces pays.

Il est de plus en plus manifeste que, dans beaucoup de PECO et pays baltes, le modèle traditionnellement applicable aux économies en transition n'est plus d'actualité. Ceux qui entrent aujourd'hui dans l'Union européenne sont peut-être davantage dans la situation des pays à revenu intermédiaire. Les autres tomberaient plus dans la catégorie des pays très endettés, des pays sortant d'un conflit ou des pays à faible revenu en difficulté. Ainsi, les problèmes auxquels font face la Hongrie et la République tchèque ont peu à voir avec ceux que connaissent le Turkménistan et la République kirghize. Si le terme *transition* était utilisé pour parler de la transformation à l'économie de marché, le label *pays en transition* ne semble plus aussi approprié pour les deux premiers pays. Les enseignements tirés de cette période, que l'ampleur de la transition a plus particulièrement mis en relief, sont toutefois d'une application plus générale.

La présente évaluation passe au crible l'aide de la Banque dans cinq domaines, retenus en raison de leur importance dans les programmes de prêt de l'institution et des enseignements qu'ils pourront permettre de tirer tant pour le travail restant à effectuer dans les pays encore en transition que d'une façon plus générale. Il s'agit du dévelop-

ENGLISH

findings and recommendations.

Private Sector Development

Transforming state-dominated and -controlled economies into market-driven, private-sector-oriented economies was a major goal of the transition. This required imposing market discipline on state-owned enterprises, privatizing state assets, and encouraging new private enterprises. Bank assistance programs initially reflected the belief that privatization must occur quickly, taking advantage of limited reform "windows," and that new private owners would restructure the enterprises and provide adequate corporate governance. This sentiment also reflected the views of leading policymakers throughout the Region. In line with this approach, early Bank assistance put a lower priority on reform of regulatory, anti-monopoly, commercial, capital market, and bankruptcy regimes, the so-called "second generation" reforms; they would be pursued once a critical mass of privatized firms had appeared. Private property has become the dominant basis for productive transactions in most transition economies. But a number of countries, particularly in the CIS, have yet to establish conditions conducive to private sector development and growth, and ailing state-owned enterprises continue to drain public resources and bottle up valuable assets. In the more advanced reformers, largely in the CEB, firms have made significant progress in restructuring, but it is the entry of large numbers of new firms that is mainly responsible for the recovery and job creation.

ESPAÑOL

cado, la etiqueta de *países con economías en transición* ya no parece ser tan aplicable. Sin embargo, las enseñanzas que dejó ese período —y que han adquirido mayor relieve debido a la gran escala de la transición— pueden aplicarse a nivel más general.

Esta evaluación examina en profundidad cinco esferas de asistencia del Banco, elegidas por su importancia para el programa de financiamiento del Banco y su potencial para dejar enseñanzas útiles para lo que resta del programa de transición y, a un nivel más amplio, para el desarrollo del sector privado, la gestión de gobierno, la administración del sector público y el fortalecimiento institucional, el sector financiero, los sistemas de protección social y la energía. No analiza en profundidad todas las esferas en las que actuó el Banco. No examina la experiencia del Banco en la liberalización de los precios y el comercio, donde se han obtenido y mantenido logros importantes. Algunas esferas han sido objeto de otras evaluaciones por parte del DEO, como un análisis de la reforma de las políticas agrícolas, que detectó avances considerables en la liberalización del comercio agrícola, la reforma agraria y el desarrollo de los mercados financieros rurales, y un menor grado de progreso en las actividades de seguimiento posteriores a la privatización y la reforma de las instituciones del Estado. Otras esferas, como el comercio, están siendo analizadas en evaluaciones del DEO actualmente en curso. En las secciones siguientes se resumen las conclusiones y recomendaciones específicamente relacionadas con las cinco esferas objeto de la presente evaluación. En la úl-

FRANÇAIS

pement du secteur privé ; de la gouvernance, de la gestion du secteur public et du renforcement des institutions ; du secteur financier ; de la protection sociale ; et de l'énergie. Tous les secteurs d'intervention de la Banque n'ont donc pas été examinés en détail. Ainsi, l'action menée par la Banque pour favoriser la libéralisation des prix et du commerce, domaines dans lesquels les acquis sont importants, n'a pas été évaluée. Certains secteurs d'activité ont fait l'objet d'autres évaluations de l'OED, comme l'examen de la réforme de la politique agricole qui a fait ressortir le long chemin parcouru au plan de la libéralisation des échanges agricoles, de la réforme foncière et du développement des marchés financiers en zone rurale, et mis en évidence le travail restant à accomplir au niveau du suivi après les privatisations et de la réforme des institutions publiques. L'OED réalise actuellement des évaluations portant sur d'autres domaines, comme le commerce. Les sections qui suivent présentent une synthèse des observations et des recommandations dans chacun des cinq domaines retenus. L'ultime section est consacrée à des observations et recommandations de portée plus générale.

Développement du secteur privé

La transition avait particulièrement pour objet de transformer des économies dominées et contrôlées par l'État en économies organisées autour du secteur privé. Pour cela, il fallait soumettre les entreprises détenues par l'État à la discipline du marché, privatiser des biens pu-

ENGLISH

The Region has drawn a series of *lessons from the first ten years of transition* that support privatization as part of a broad strategy of discipline and encouragement, quick sale of small enterprises through open and competitive auctions, case-by-case privatization of medium-size and large enterprises, an enforceable legal system to protect investors, increased competition, clarification of the cash flow and property rights of enterprises with continued state ownership, and great caution, along with an efficient regulatory regime, in divesting enterprises in sectors characterized by natural monopoly or oligopoly. *OED's findings are consistent with these lessons. Moreover, with the benefit of hindsight, OED considers that the Bank should have pursued this agenda sooner than it did.* In the earliest years of the transition, many of the choices made by the Bank were probably appropriate, given what was known at the time. However, by the mid-1990s, it is reasonable to ask whether the Bank was focusing sufficiently on the climate for private sector development (PSD) and the appropriate methods for disciplining and privatizing medium-size and large enterprises.

Governance, Public Sector Management, and Institution Building

At the beginning of the transition, the Bank understood the need to reorient and strengthen public sector institutions, but it greatly underestimated the consequences of still weak core institutions and public administrations managing the transition process. Work in the Bank

ESPAÑOL

tima sección se exponen algunas conclusiones y recomendaciones intersectoriales.

Desarrollo del sector privado

Uno de los objetivos principales de la transición fue transformar economías dominadas y controladas por el Estado en economías impulsadas por el mercado y orientadas al sector privado. Para ello fue necesario imponer una disciplina de mercado a empresas estatales, privatizar bienes del Estado y estimular la creación de nuevas empresas privadas. Los programas de asistencia del Banco reflejaron, al principio, la creencia de que las privatizaciones debían hacerse con rapidez, aprovechando las escasas oportunidades de introducir reformas, y de que los nuevos propietarios privados reestructurarían las empresas y harían una buena gestión de gobierno empresarial. Este sentimiento también reflejó las opiniones de las autoridades encargadas de formular las políticas en toda la región. De conformidad con este criterio, la asistencia del Banco en la etapa inicial asignó una menor prioridad a la reforma de los regímenes regulatorios, antimonopólicos, comerciales, del mercado de capitales y de quiebra, es decir, las llamadas reformas "de segunda generación", las que se aplicarían una vez que hubiera surgido una masa crítica de empresas privatizadas. La propiedad privada se ha convertido en la base principal de las transacciones productivas en la mayoría de los países con economías en transición. Pero en algunos países, en particular de la CEI, aún no han se han creado las condiciones favorables para el desarrollo del sector privado y el crecimiento, y hay empresas estatales

FRANÇAIS

blics et encourager la création d'entreprises privées. Au début, les programmes d'aide de la Banque reposaient sur la conviction que la privatisation devait intervenir rapidement, pour tirer parti des rares « fenêtres » de réforme, et que les nouveaux détenteurs du capital restructuraient leurs sociétés et mettraient en place le type de gouvernement d'entreprise voulu. Les dirigeants de la région partageaient ce sentiment. Aussi l'aide initiale de la Banque n'a-t-elle pas mis l'accent sur la réforme des dispositifs régissant le cadre réglementaire et commercial, la lutte contre les monopoles, les marchés financiers et les faillites, des réformes dites de la « seconde génération ». Celles-ci ne seraient entreprises qu'après l'émergence d'une masse critique d'entreprises privatisées. Dans la plupart des pays en transition, la propriété privée est aujourd'hui l'axe central des transactions productives. Mais, un certain nombre de pays, surtout dans le CEI, doivent encore créer les conditions propices au développement du secteur privé et à la croissance, et faire en sorte que les entreprises d'État en perte de vitesse cessent de continuer à ponctionner les ressources publiques et à immobiliser de précieux actifs. Dans les pays où les réformes sont plus avancées, principalement dans les PECO et les pays baltes, la restructuration des sociétés a beaucoup progressé, mais la reprise et la création d'emplois sont surtout dues à l'entrée sur le marché d'un grand nombre de nouvelles entreprises.

La Région a tiré un ensemble *d'enseignements des 10 premières années de la transition*. Ces ensei-

ENGLISH

in the early 1990s recognized the quality of governance as an appropriate matter for Bank attention, but the Bank as a whole had few specialists in governance and public sector management (PSM) reform at that time. Despite large transfers of resources from the Bank to the transition countries, little analysis of public expenditures was undertaken before the late 1990s. Toward the end of the decade, pioneering work by the Bank's ECA Region and surveys by the Bank, the European Bank for Reconstruction and Development (EBRD), and others documented pervasive corruption and massive diversion of public resources in the Region. This work highlighted *the importance of confronting corruption, an issue that had previously been taboo for the Bank, as well as the need to link public expenditure analysis with the broader issues of public financial accountability,* on which reporting is now mandatory. Almost all recent transition Country Assistance Strategies (CASs) place PSM reform at the center of assistance strategy, and this has been reflected in projects. *Transparency is a key to increasing public accountability and discouraging corruption,* and while the Bank has increased its focus on promoting a culture of transparency, more emphasis is warranted.

Rule of law, including judicial reform, is critical to building successful democratic market-based economic systems. The record in this area throughout the Bank has been disappointing. Evaluations suggest that while the majority of laws supported by the Bank have been submitted or passed, projects have not yet met

ESPAÑOL

cargadas de problemas que siguen drenando recursos públicos y reteniendo activos valiosos. En los países que más han avanzado en las reformas, principalmente los países de Europa central y oriental y del Báltico, las empresas han hecho grandes progresos en cuanto a su reestructuración, pero la entrada de un gran número de empresas nuevas es la principal responsable de la recuperación económica y la generación de empleos.

La región ha recogido una serie de *enseñanzas de los primeros diez años de transición* que respaldan la privatización como parte de una estrategia amplia de disciplina y estímulo, la venta rápida de pequeñas empresas en subastas abiertas y competitivas, la privatización caso por caso de las empresas grandes y medianas, un sistema jurídico con garantías de cumplimiento para proteger a los inversores, una mayor competencia, la aclaración del flujo de efectivo y los derechos de propiedad de las empresas que siguen siendo total o parcialmente de propiedad del Estado, y mucha cautela, unida a un régimen regulatorio eficiente, al privatizar empresas de sectores caracterizados por monopolios u oligopolios naturales. *Las conclusiones del DEO concuerdan con estas enseñanzas. Además, en retrospectiva, el DEO considera que el Banco debería haber puesto en marcha su programa más tempranamente.* En los primeros años de la transición, muchas de las decisiones que tomó el Banco fueron probablemente apropiadas, habida cuenta de lo que se sabía en aquel momento. Sin embargo, para mediados del decenio de 1990, es razonable preguntarse si el Banco estaba prestando la

FRANÇAIS

gnements militent en faveur de la privatisation dans le cadre d'une stratégie globale de discipline et de promotion des entreprises, de la vente rapide aux enchères publiques des petites entreprises, de la privatisation au cas par cas des moyennes et grandes entreprises, de l'adoption d'un système juridique applicable pour protéger les investisseurs, du renforcement de la concurrence, de la présentation dénuée d'ambiguïté de la trésorerie et des droits patrimoniaux des entreprises toujours sous le contrôle de l'État, et d'une grande prudence, doublée d'un régime réglementaire approprié, lors des désétatisations dans des secteurs caractérisés par une situation de monopole naturel ou d'oligopole. *L'OED parvient aux mêmes conclusions. En outre, avec le recul, l'OED considère que la Banque aurait dû s'engager sur cette voie plus tôt.* Au cours des premières années de la transition, beaucoup des choix faits par la Banque étaient certainement justifiés, compte tenu de l'état des connaissances à l'époque. Toutefois, à partir du milieu des années 90, on peut légitimement se demander si la Banque s'est suffisamment attachée à promouvoir l'émergence d'un climat favorisant le développement du secteur privé et l'adoption des mesures nécessaires pour discipliner et privatiser les moyennes et grandes entreprises.

Gouvernance, gestion du secteur public et renforcement des institutions

Au début de la transition, la Banque a compris qu'il fallait réorienter et renforcer les institutions du secteur public, mais elle a beaucoup sous-es-

ENGLISH

their broader objective of systemic change. *PSM reform has often been approached in an ad hoc manner, without a comprehensive long-term institutional development and reform strategy.*

Financial Sector

At the outset, transition economies possessed financial systems whose basic purpose was to allocate funds according to the plan, with a limited capacity to intermediate financial resources and no need for prudential regulations or financial supervision. The Bank, in close collaboration with the IMF, quickly formed a basic understanding of the essential elements of financial sector transition, and these elements—macroeconomic stability, legal and regulatory frameworks, and accounting systems, with an emphasis on the banking sector—were repeated in most countries with active programs. Most transition economies have made tangible progress toward market-based financial systems. However, some of the analyses and assistance efforts did not take into account the interrelationships between banking sector and enterprise reform, and allowed the process to be subverted by managers and interlocking owners. Privately owned banks strongly interlinked with major borrowing enterprises make poor candidates for sound and efficient intermediation. *Measures are needed at an early stage to enforce prudential regulations, including limits on loan concentration and related-party lending, and Bank projects should be conditioned on such measures.* While substantial privatization has taken place, *banks under*

ESPAÑOL

suficiente atención a la existencia de un clima favorable para el desarrollo del sector privado y a los métodos apropiados para disciplinar y privatizar empresas medianas y grandes.

Gestión de gobierno, administración del sector público y fortalecimiento institucional

Al comienzo de la transición, el Banco entendió la necesidad de reorientar y fortalecer a las instituciones del sector público, pero subestimó excesivamente las consecuencias de dejar en manos de instituciones centrales y administraciones públicas aún débiles la conducción del proceso de transición. En trabajos realizados por el Banco a principios de los años noventa se reconoció que la calidad de la gestión de gobierno era un asunto que requería la atención del Banco, pero en aquel momento el Banco en su conjunto tenía pocos especialistas en la reforma de la gestión de gobierno y la administración del sector público. A pesar de las voluminosas transferencias de recursos del Banco a los países en transición, el gasto público no fue objeto de mayores análisis hasta fines del decenio de 1990. Hacia el final de la década, trabajos de vanguardia de la Oficina Regional de Europa y Asia Central del Banco y estudios realizados por el Banco Europeo de Reconstrucción y Fomento (BERF) y otras entidades, documentaron que la corrupción y la desviación de recursos públicos eran moneda corriente en la región. Este trabajo puso de relieve *la importancia de hacer frente a la corrupción, un tema que hasta entonces había sido tabú para el Banco, así como la necesidad de vincular el análisis del*

FRANÇAIS

timé les conséquences que pouvait avoir la situation encore fragile d'administrations publiques et d'institutions de base chargées de piloter le processus. Au début des années 90, elle n'ignorait pas que la qualité de la gouvernance devait s'inscrire dans le cadre de son action, mais l'institution comptait à cette époque peu de spécialistes de cette question et de la réforme de la gestion du secteur public. Bien que la Banque ait transféré un important volume de ressources vers les pays en transition, aucune analyse détaillée des dépenses publiques n'a été entreprise avant la fin des années 90, époque à laquelle des travaux innovants de la Région ECA et des études de l'institution, de la Banque européenne pour la reconstruction et le développement (BERD) et d'autres organismes ont mis en évidence une corruption généralisée et des détournements massifs de ressources publiques dans la région. Ce travail a montré *combien il était important de s'attaquer à la corruption, une question jusque-là taboue à la Banque, et de replacer l'analyse des dépenses publiques dans le cadre plus large de la question de l'éthique de responsabilité financière des pouvoirs publics*, un aspect qui fait aujourd'hui systématiquement l'objet d'un rapport. Les récentes stratégies d'aide aux pays (CAS) en transition s'organisent presque toutes autour de la réforme du secteur public, comme en témoignent les projets mis en œuvre. *Le renforcement de l'éthique de responsabilité financière des pouvoirs publics et les mesures dissuasives en matière de corruption passent nécessairement par la transpa-*

ENGLISH

state ownership still need strengthening, through stronger governance, tighter budget constraints, divestiture of branches, and restrictions on the scope of banking licenses.

Bank assistance programs have appropriately emphasized the establishment of a proper legal and regulatory framework for the financial sector, but the time and human resource development required to make the new laws and regulations effective were underestimated. Training was provided to project implementation units, to financial intermediaries participating in Bank credit lines, and to the restructuring and privatization agencies. Few resources were devoted to the extended training needed to operate the financial system as a whole. *High priority should be given to training bank supervisors, lawyers and judges, accountants and auditors, and other skilled professionals. Progress in increasing the effectiveness of bank supervision and in enforcing (not just adopting) international accounting standards should be among the triggers for lending.*

Close to half of operations with financial sector components in the transition economies included lines of credit, many of them in sectors other than finance, and their outcome ratings have been low: fewer than half the commitments in the financial, rural, social protection, and PSD sectors were rated satisfactory. Few of them treated the financial sustainability of the intermediaries as a key objective. Moreover, the underlying assumption that credit would be a binding constraint on PSD in the early transition experi-

ESPAÑOL

gasto público a la cuestión más amplia de la rendición de cuentas en el sector de las finanzas públicas, en el que la presentación de informes es actualmente obligatoria. Casi todas las Estrategias de asistencia a países en transición elaboradas recientemente colocan a la reforma de la administración del sector público en el centro de la estrategia de asistencia, y esto se ha reflejado en los proyectos. *La transparencia es un factor clave para mejorar la rendición de cuentas en el sector público y desalentar la corrupción,* y si bien el Banco está asignando mayor prioridad a la promoción de una cultura de transparencia, el tema amerita un énfasis mayor.

El estado de derecho, incluida la reforma judicial, es fundamental para el éxito de los sistemas económicos democráticos basados en el mercado. Los logros del Banco en esa esfera han sido decepcionantes. Las evaluaciones sugieren que si bien la mayoría de las leyes que han recibido el apoyo del Banco han sido propuestas o aprobadas, los proyectos no han logrado aún su objetivo más amplio de cambio sistémico. *La reforma de la administración del sector público a menudo se ha encarado según las necesidades particulares del caso, y no en el marco de una estrategia institucional amplia y a largo plazo de desarrollo y reforma.*

Sector financiero

Al comienzo, los países con economías en transición tenían sistemas financieros cuyo objetivo básico era asignar los fondos de acuerdo con el plan, con una capacidad limitada para actuar como intermediarios de recursos financieros y sin necesidad de

FRANÇAIS

rence. Si la Banque s'attache aujourd'hui davantage à promouvoir une culture de la transparence, plus doit encore être fait dans ce domaine.

L'état de droit, qui suppose une réforme judiciaire, est à la base de tout bon système économique démocratique fondé sur le jeu du marché. Dans ce domaine, les résultats obtenus par la Banque sont décevants. Les évaluations réalisées tendent à montrer que la majorité des lois appuyées par la Banque ont bien été présentées ou adoptées, mais que les projets n'ont pas atteint leur objectif plus large de changement systémique. *La réforme de la gestion du secteur public est souvent abordée de façon décousue, alors qu'elle devrait s'inscrire dans une stratégie globale de développement et de réforme des institutions à long terme.*

Le secteur financier

Au départ, les systèmes financiers des pays en transition avaient principalement pour objet de répartir les financements conformément au plan ; leurs capacités ne leur permettaient pas de jouer un rôle d'intermédiaire susceptible d'apporter des ressources financières et ils n'étaient soumis ni à une réglementation prudentielle, ni à une supervision financière. La Banque mondiale, travaillant en étroite collaboration avec le FMI, est rapidement parvenue à isoler quels étaient les principaux éléments de la transition du secteur financier, et ces éléments — stabilité macroéconomique, cadres juridiques et réglementaires et systèmes comptables, appliqués tout particulièrement au

ENGLISH

ence can be questioned in hindsight, as the utilization of credit lines was far less than anticipated. *Financial sector staff should be involved in the design of all financial intermediary loans and should ensure that the factors important to sustainability are adequately taken into account. Microfinance projects should give greater attention to developing savings services and should incorporate from the start a donor exit strategy.*

Capital markets development was sometimes overemphasized in the early years of the transition, both within and outside the Bank, and it may have diverted attention from more immediate concerns, and scarce regulatory and supervisory resources from the banking system. No formal stock market could have played the role assigned to it by the mass privatization proponents without a properly functioning banking system, adequate accounting and auditing with effective disclosure requirements, responsible corporate governance, and protections for minority shareholders.

Social Protection

Reform of the social protection system in transition countries was initially viewed as a means to cushion the impact of the structural reforms. Early operations concentrated on helping employment services deal with the expected surge of displaced workers. Job displacements proved fewer than anticipated, however, and slow growth of alternative employment opportunities undermined retraining efforts. Moreover, insufficient attention was given to the longer-term problem of people

ESPAÑOL

normas reglamentarias prudentes o supervisión financiera. El Banco, en estrecha colaboración con el FMI, se formó rápidamente un concepto básico de los elementos esenciales de la transición del sector financiero, y esos elementos —estabilidad macroeconómica, marcos jurídicos y regulatorios y sistemas de contabilidad, con un énfasis en el sector bancario— se repitieron en la mayoría de los países con programas activos. La mayoría de los países con economías en transición han hecho progresos tangibles con miras a la implantación de sistemas financieros basados en el mercado. Sin embargo, algunos de los análisis y medidas de asistencia no tuvieron en cuenta las interrelaciones existentes entre el sector bancario y la reforma de las empresas, y permitieron que el proceso fuera socavado por administradores y propietarios con intereses superpuestos. Los bancos de propiedad privada vinculados muy estrechamente a grandes empresas prestatarias no eran buenos candidatos para ejercer una intermediación racional y eficiente. *Es necesario adoptar medidas en una etapa temprana para aplicar normas reglamentarias prudentes, que entre otras cosas limiten la concentración de préstamos y la concesión de financiamiento a partes vinculadas, y los proyectos del Banco deberían condicionarse a la observancia de estas medidas.* Si bien ha habido un gran número de privatizaciones, *es preciso fortalecer aún más los bancos estatales, mediante una gestión de gobierno más sólida, restricciones presupuestarias más estrictas, privatización de las sucursales y limitación del alcance de las licencias bancarias.*

FRANÇAIS

secteur bancaire — ont été reproduits dans la plupart des pays ayant des programmes en activité. Dans la plupart des pays en transition, on observe des progrès tangibles vers la mise en place de systèmes financiers obéissant aux lois du marché. Toutefois, certains des efforts déployés en matière d'analyse et d'aide n'ont pas pris en considération les liens d'interdépendance qui existaient entre secteur bancaire et entreprises faisant l'objet de réformes, ce qui a permis aux directeurs et aux propriétaires de sociétés aux directions imbriquées de détourner le processus de son objectif. Du fait de leurs prises de participations non négligeables dans les entreprises auxquelles elles accordent des prêts importants, les banques privées sont mal placées pour s'acquitter avec pertinence et efficacité du rôle d'intermédiation que l'on attend d'elles. *Il faut que des mesures d'exécution des réglementations prudentielles soient prises très rapidement, notamment celles qui concernent les limites à la concentration des prêts et les prêts consentis à des parties liées, et les projets de la Banque mondiale devraient être subordonnés à l'existence de telles mesures.* Il y a eu un mouvement de privatisation important *mais il faut encore renforcer les banques qui sont placées sous le contrôle de l'État et dans cette optique, il y a lieu de renforcer leur gouvernance, de leur imposer des contraintes budgétaires plus strictes, de les amener à se désengager de leurs succursales et il faut également imposer des restrictions au champ d'activités des institutions bancaires agréées.*

ENGLISH

too old to be retrained or to find new jobs, which resulted in declining revenues and growing expenditures for early retirement and disability programs. Financial difficulties in pension programs became major fiscal problems in most countries, while deteriorating economies caused sharp increases in poverty rates, exposing the weaknesses in existing social assistance programs.

The Bank's emphasis shifted to pensions, where it helped many countries—through technical assistance as much as lending—enact major reforms. However, the existence of two alternative models for reform led to disagreements among international agencies, as well as within the Bank, and probably delayed reforms in some countries. In others, it led to the premature adoption of multi-pillar systems, with too little attention to the fiscal sustainability of the basic pension system and to the capacity to meet the preconditions for a private pension system. *A clear strategic approach to pension reform is needed, differentiated by the ability of the country to administer and fund the system.*

The weakest link in the Bank's social protection reform strategy was in developing country-level agendas. This resulted in missed opportunities, particularly in social assistance benefits for the poor, to which the Bank did not devote the same kind of resources as it did to pension reform. Too great a share of benefits—such as child allowances and subsidized services—are directed to higher-income households. Those in poorer regions of a country find it difficult to qualify for ben-

ESPAÑOL

Los programas de asistencia del Banco han puesto el debido énfasis en la creación de un marco jurídico y regulatorio adecuado para el sector financiero, pero se subestimó el tiempo y el grado de capacitación de los recursos humanos que se requeriría para poner en práctica las nuevas leyes y reglamentaciones. Se impartió capacitación a las unidades de ejecución de proyectos, a los intermediarios financieros que participaban en las líneas de crédito del Banco, y a los organismos de reestructuración y privatización. Se destinaron pocos recursos a la amplia capacitación necesaria para hacer funcionar el sistema financiero en su conjunto. *Debería asignarse alta prioridad a la capacitación de supervisores de los bancos, abogados y jueces, contadores y auditores y otros profesionales idóneos. Los progresos alcanzados en cuanto a aumentar la eficacia de la supervisión de los bancos y de la aplicación (no solamente de la adopción) de normas internacionales de contabilidad deberían ser uno de los mecanismos activadores del financiamiento.*

Cerca de la mitad de las operaciones con componentes del sector financiero en los países con economías en transición incluyeron líneas de crédito, muchas de ellas en sectores distintos del financiero, y sus resultados han sido calificados de pobres: menos de la mitad de los compromisos asumidos en los sectores financiero, rural, de la protección social y de desarrollo del sector privado fueron calificados de satisfactorios. Pocos de ellos encararon la sostenibilidad financiera de los intermediarios como un objetivo clave. Además, en retrospectiva, la presunción subyacente de que el

FRANÇAIS

Les programmes d'aide de la Banque mondiale ont, à juste titre, mis l'accent sur la création d'un cadre juridique et réglementaire adapté qui puisse être appliqué au secteur financier mais ils ont sous-estimé le temps qu'il fallait pour que ces nouvelles lois et réglementations entrent en vigueur et les qualifications professionnelles requises à l'appui d'une telle démarche. Une formation a été offerte au personnel des unités d'exécution de projets, aux intermédiaires financiers participant aux lignes de crédit de la Banque, et au personnel des organismes de restructuration et de privatisation. On n'a pas consacré de ressources suffisantes à l'offre d'une formation de longue durée pourtant nécessaire à l'exploitation de l'ensemble du système financier. *La formation des personnes chargées d'exercer une surveillance bancaire, des avocats et des juges, des experts-comptables et des auditeurs, et d'autres professionnels qualifiés, doit bénéficier d'un rang élevé de priorité. L'octroi de prêts devrait être subordonné à la réalisation de progrès dans l'efficacité de la surveillance bancaire et dans la mise en application (et non pas seulement dans l'adoption) de normes comptables internationales.*

Dans les économies en transition, près de la moitié des opérations ayant une composante liée au secteur financier porte sur des lignes de crédit, dont beaucoup se rapportent à des secteurs autres que le secteur financier et la notation des résultats obtenus de cette manière laisse à désirer : moins de la moitié des engagements dans les secteurs financiers et ruraux, ainsi que dans les domaines de la protection so-

ENGLISH

efits, and they receive less; and benefit levels are too low to be of much use in fighting poverty. Lending tended to neglect administrative reforms, often because the borrowers did not want to pay for technical assistance, and both pension and other social assistance programs suffer from administrative shortcomings. *Greater attention should now go to strengthening the capacity of national institutions to analyze needs, develop a policy consensus, improve collections, and administer benefits.*

In retrospect, the Bank should have addressed *additional areas that have proven to be barriers to social protection reform in virtually every transition economy*—labor laws that encourage labor hoarding among declining firms and discourage hiring among expanding firms, strategies for sharing fiscal and policy burdens of assistance programs among different levels of government, and problems in coverage and administration caused by the growth of informal sectors.

Energy

The transition countries inherited substantial energy infrastructure, consisting of vertically integrated public monopolies. Energy consumption and production were heavily subsidized, while customer service was inadequate, and facilities poorly maintained. Supply-side problems were exacerbated by low efficiency of consumption, a lack of metering, and unwillingness to pay. None of the regulatory or institutional arrangements necessary for commercial operations was in place, and there were serious environmental problems.

ESPAÑOL

crédito sería una restricción forzosa para el desarrollo del sector privado en la primera etapa de la transición es cuestionable, ya que la utilización de las líneas de crédito fue mucho menor de lo que se esperaba. *El personal del sector financiero debería participar en el diseño de todos los préstamos de intermediación financiera y asegurarse de que se tomen debidamente en cuenta los factores importantes para la sostenibilidad. Los proyectos de microfinanciamiento deberían prestar mayor atención al desarrollo de los servicios de ahorro y deberían incorporar desde el comienzo una estrategia referente a la retirada de los donantes.*

En los primeros años de la transición se puso a veces un énfasis excesivo en el desarrollo de los mercados de capitales tanto dentro como fuera del Banco, lo que puede haber desviado la atención de problemas más inmediatos y sustraído del sistema bancario parte de los escasos recursos de regulación y supervisión. Ningún mercado de valores oficial podría haber desempeñado el papel que le asignaron los proponentes de las privatizaciones en masa sin contar con un sistema bancario que funcionara correctamente, un sistema adecuado de contabilidad y auditoría regido por normas de libre acceso a la información, un gobierno empresarial responsable y medidas de protección de los accionistas minoritarios.

Protección social

La reforma del sistema de protección social en los países en transición se encaró inicialmente como un medio de amortiguar los efectos de las reformas estructurales. Las medidas

FRANÇAIS

ciale et du développement du secteur privé ont été jugés satisfaisants. Rares sont les opérations qui faisaient de la viabilité financière des intermédiaires un objectif clé. De plus, rétrospectivement, il semble que l'on puisse douter du bien fondé de l'hypothèse de départ selon laquelle le crédit serait une contrainte incontournable pour le développement du secteur privé au début de la phase de transition, puisque les lignes de crédit ont été utilisées de façon moins systématique que prévu. *Les services du secteur financier devraient être impliqués davantage dans la conception de tous les prêts intermédiaires et devraient veiller à ce que les facteurs qui jouent un rôle important sur le plan de la viabilité soient suffisamment pris en compte. Les projets de microfinancement devraient accorder plus d'importance à la mise en place de services d'épargne et incorporer dès l'origine une stratégie de désengagement des bailleurs de fonds.*

Au cours des premières années de la transition, on a peut-être prêté trop d'importance, au sein de la Banque mondiale et à l'extérieur, au développement des marchés financiers et cela au détriment de préoccupations plus immédiates comme l'insuffisance des ressources pouvant être affectées à la réglementation et à la supervision du secteur bancaire. Aucun marché boursier officiel n'aurait pu jouer le rôle qu'auraient voulu lui assigner les partisans des privatisations de masse, en l'absence d'un système bancaire fonctionnel, de systèmes comptables et d'audit satisfaisants, de mesures efficaces de diffusion de l'information au grand public, d'une gouvernance

ENGLISH

The Bank's initial policy on lending for electric power linked Bank support to reforms in commercialization, corporatization, and arm's-length regulation. By 1996, the Bank had adopted an approach that emphasized unbundling and privatization to achieve commercialization. *Rehabilitation, emergency relief, and critical imports projects,* which accounted for over one-third of energy projects, encountered difficulties because of procurement problems and conflicts between short- and long-run objectives; such projects *should be designed to minimize delays (use negative lists rather than trying to pre-identify critical imports) and forego project implementation units and long-term reform objectives.* Nearly two-thirds of energy projects focused on longer-term objectives, and satisfactory outcomes tended to result from a programmatic approach, with a blend of adjustment and investment operations, accompanied by analytical work. This was also an effective way to include issues beyond the scope of energy sector lending, such as the elimination of subsidies to energy sector entities; increased discipline in metering, billing, and collecting payments; reforming pricing policies; and closing uneconomic energy production facilities. Stakeholder participation proved effective in some cases, such as the privatization of Russian coal mines. In other cases, progress was limited. Efforts to integrate environmental concerns were generally effective.

In retrospect, probably too much emphasis was given to privatization and restructuring, and too little to regulation, strengthening utility fi-

ESPAÑOL

iniciales se centraron en ayudar a los servicios de empleo a lidiar con la oleada prevista de trabajadores desplazados. Sin embargo, el desplazamiento de empleos fue menor al esperado, y el lento crecimiento de otras oportunidades de empleo menoscabó los esfuerzos de readiestramiento. Además, no se prestó suficiente atención al problema a más largo plazo de la gente que ya tenía demasiada edad como para volver a capacitarse o encontrar nuevos empleos, lo que trajo aparejada una disminución de los ingresos y un aumento de los gastos de los programas de jubilación anticipada e incapacidad. Las dificultades financieras de los programas de pensiones se convirtieron en graves problemas fiscales en la mayoría de los países, al tiempo que el deterioro de las economías provocó un fuerte aumento de las tasas de pobreza, dejando al descubierto las deficiencias de los programas de asistencia social existentes.

El Banco dirigió entonces su atención al sistema de pensiones, sector en el que ayudó a muchos países — mediante asistencia técnica y préstamos— a aprobar reformas sustanciales. Sin embargo, la existencia de dos modelos de reforma distintos dio lugar a desacuerdos entre los organismos internacionales, así como dentro del Banco, y probablemente retrasó las reformas en algunos países. En otros, llevó a la adopción prematura de sistemas de pilares múltiples, que no tenían demasiado en cuenta la sostenibilidad fiscal del sistema básico de pensiones y la capacidad de cumplir las condiciones previas necesarias para la creación de un sistema privado de pensiones. *Se requiere un claro en-*

FRANÇAIS

responsable des entreprises et d'un système de protection des actionnaires minoritaires.

Protection sociale

La réforme du système de protection sociale dans les pays en transition était envisagée initialement comme un moyen d'atténuer l'impact des réformes structurelles. Les premières opérations ont surtout visé à aider les services de l'emploi à faire face à l'augmentation attendue du nombre de travailleurs licenciés. Toutefois, les suppressions d'emplois ont été moins importantes que prévu et la création de postes de substitution n'a pas suivi le rythme attendu, ce qui a miné les efforts déployés pour offrir une formation de reconversion. En outre, il n'a pas été prêté suffisamment d'attention au problème que posent, à long terme, les personnes trop âgées pour bénéficier d'une formation de reconversion ou pour trouver de nouveaux emplois, ce qui s'est traduit par une baisse des recettes et une augmentation des dépenses au titre de retraites anticipées et de programmes d'invalidité. Les difficultés financières que posaient les programmes de retraites se sont converties, dans la plupart des pays, en de graves problèmes budgétaires tandis que la dégradation des économies provoquait une forte augmentation des taux de pauvreté, révélant ainsi les faiblesses des programmes existants d'assistance sociale.

La Banque mondiale a fait porter plus particulièrement ses efforts sur les retraites et elle a aidé de nombreux pays à mettre en œuvre d'importantes réformes dans ce domaine, par le biais d'une assis-

nancial and managerial performance, and combating corruption. As the ECA Region has noted, attempts to leap from noncommercial, state-owned entities to private commercial utilities generally failed, although in some cases (Kazakhstan and some CEB countries) they brought sector improvements (falling subsidies, for example), and even where this approach was not fully successful, service quality and coverage have tended to improve. EU accession is a strong motivating factor for some countries, but in many others it was unrealistic to expect restructuring and privatization to overcome legal, political, structural, and attitudinal obstacles. *The primary objectives for enterprises in the energy sector should be improved commercial performance and corporate and sectoral governance. The sequencing of reforms, including the feasibility of immediate privatization, depends on country circumstances. The Bank needs to develop operational guidance as to what sequence of reforms and interventions works best in particular country situations.*

Crosscutting Findings and Recommendations

Bank teams starting work in countries in the ECA transition group, with limited prior knowledge of these countries, were often forced to engage in assistance programs without the luxury of careful analysis. With the benefit of hindsight, OED's findings and recommendations based on this tumultuous period of economic, social, and political change are meant to help guide many of the Bank's policy precepts and procedures. With this in mind,

foque estratégico de la reforma del sistema de pensiones, que varíe según la capacidad de cada país para administrar y financiar el sistema.

El eslabón más débil de la estrategia de reforma del sistema de protección social del Banco fue la elaboración de programas a nivel de los países en desarrollo. Ello dio lugar a que se desaprovecharan oportunidades, particularmente en lo que respecta a otorgar beneficios de asistencia social a los pobres, a los cuales el Banco no destinó el mismo volumen de recursos que a la reforma del sistema de pensiones. Una proporción excesiva de los beneficios —como las prestaciones por hijos a cargo y servicios subsidiados— está dirigida a los hogares de ingresos más altos. Las personas que viven en las regiones más pobres de un país a menudo tienen dificultades para acceder a los beneficios y reciben menos; y la cuantía de las prestaciones es demasiado baja como para ser de gran ayuda en la lucha contra la pobreza. El financiamiento tendió a descuidar las reformas administrativas, con frecuencia porque los prestatarios se negaban a pagar la asistencia técnica, y tanto los sistemas de pensiones como otros programas de asistencia social adolecen de deficiencias administrativas. *Actualmente debería prestarse más atención al fortalecimiento de la capacidad de las instituciones nacionales para analizar las necesidades, generar un consenso en torno a las políticas, mejorar la recaudación y administrar las prestaciones.*

En retrospectiva, el Banco debería haberse ocupado también de *otras esferas que han demostrado ser ba-*

tance technique tout autant que par ses prêts. Cependant, le fait que deux modèles de réformes aient été en présence s'est traduit par des désaccords entre les organismes internationaux et au sein de la Banque mondiale, et a probablement retardé la mise en œuvre des réformes dans certains pays. Dans d'autres pays, cela a conduit à l'adoption prématurée d'un régime à plusieurs piliers, et l'on a pas prêté suffisamment attention à la viabilité budgétaire du régime de base des retraites, pas plus que l'on ne s'est préoccupé de savoir s'il existait des capacités suffisantes pour satisfaire aux conditions préalables d'un système de retraites privé. *Il faut arrêter une stratégie claire en matière de réforme des retraites, et prévoir de différencier cette stratégie en fonction de l'aptitude du pays à administrer et à financer un tel régime.*

Le maillon le plus faible dans la stratégie de réforme de la protection sociale proposée par la Banque mondiale, tenait à ce que les programmes n'étaient pas mis au point au niveau de chaque pays. Il en est résulté bien des occasions manquées notamment au plan des prestations d'aide sociale destinées aux pauvres, un domaine auquel la Banque n'a pas consacré autant de ressources qu'à la réforme du système de retraites. Une trop grande part des prestations sociales — notamment les allocations familiales et les services subventionnés — vise des ménages à revenus plus élevés. Les habitants des régions pauvres d'un pays ont du mal à faire valoir leurs droits à des prestations et ils touchent des sommes moins importantes ; le niveau de ces prestations

ENGLISH

we present a number of findings that cut across sectors and lend themselves to recommendations that are broadly applicable, not only to the transition countries, but to many others as well:

- When the Bank begins work for the first time in a country—or after a long hiatus, when the country knowledge needs updating—*prudent levels of lending* are advisable until better *knowledge* is built up and greater *certainty regarding ownership* of programs can be perceived.

- Experience in countries such as Poland and Russia (coal restructuring) and Bulgaria (pension reform) shows that however well designed a reform, its rate of progress is largely determined by the government's ownership of it and the degree of consensus it is able to mobilize in the society at large. A well-informed civil society can become a major "driver" for change. Programs to *generate stakeholder awareness and participation* should be replicated widely.

- Country assistance strategies, particularly where reform progress has been slow, should promote government ownership and consensus in favor of reform through *capacity building* for both government and civil society. They should incorporate an analysis of the underlying political and social, as well as economic, processes that affect stakeholder behavior.

- An appropriate institutional and regulatory framework and a capable, transparent public sector are key elements of an efficient market-oriented private sector. *Analytical*

ESPAÑOL

rreras para la reforma de los sistemas de protección social en prácticamente todos los países con economías en transición, como leyes laborales que fomentan la acumulación de trabajadores en empresas en decadencia y desalientan la contratación por parte de empresas en expansión, estrategias para distribuir la carga fiscal y normativa de los programas de asistencia entre distintos niveles de gobierno, y problemas de cobertura y administración causados por el crecimiento de los sectores no estructurados de la economía.

Energía

Los países en transición heredaron una importante infraestructura energética, compuesta de monopolios públicos integrados verticalmente. El consumo y la producción de energía estaban fuertemente subsidiados, mientras que los servicios brindados a los usuarios eran inadecuados y las instalaciones no estaban bien mantenidas. Los problemas relacionados con el suministro se vieron agravados por la baja eficiencia del consumo, la falta de medición y la falta de voluntad de pago. No existía ninguno de los mecanismos regulatorios o institucionales necesarios para las operaciones comerciales, y había graves problemas ambientales.

La política inicial del Banco en materia de préstamos para el sector de la energía eléctrica condicionó el apoyo del Banco a las reformas de la reglamentación relativa a la comercialización, la creación de sociedades y la regulación por órganos independientes. Para 1996, el Banco había adoptado un criterio que hacía hincapié en la desagregación y la privatización para lograr la comerciali-

FRANÇAIS

n'est pas suffisant pour permettre de lutter utilement contre la pauvreté. De façon générale, les prêts n'étaient pas octroyés au titre de réformes administratives, parce qu'il arrivait souvent que les emprunteurs ne veuillent pas payer l'assistance technique et de ce fait, les programmes de retraite aussi bien que les programmes d'aide sociale ont à pâtir des lacunes administratives. *Il y a lieu maintenant d'accorder une plus grande attention au renforcement des capacités dont disposent les institutions nationales pour analyser les besoins, parvenir à un consensus politique, améliorer les rentrées de fonds et administrer les prestations.*

Rétrospectivement, la Banque aurait dû s'attaquer à *d'autres domaines faisant obstacle à la réforme de la protection sociale dans pratiquement toutes les économies en transition* — le droit du travail, qui favorise la rétention de main d'œuvre dans les entreprises en déclin et décourage le recrutement par les entreprises en expansion, les stratégies de répartition, entre différents niveaux de gouvernement, des charges budgétaires et politiques qu'implique ces programmes d'aide, et les problèmes de couverture et d'administration posés par la croissance des secteurs informels.

Énergie

Les pays en transition ont hérité d'une importante infrastructure énergétique constituée de monopoles d'État intégrés verticalement. Consommation et production d'énergie étaient fortement subventionnées, mais les services aux consommateurs étaient inadaptés

ENGLISH

work on governance and public sector management needs to precede large amounts of Bank lending, particularly when obvious problems are likely to affect assistance programs. *A comprehensive, long-term approach* is needed in developing strategies for institutional change and public sector management reform.

- *Legal and judicial reform is critical* for improvements in the business climate (company, security, bankruptcy, and anti-monopoly laws; respect for private property, contractual rights), the financial sector (banking and central banking, collateral, failed bank resolution), social protection (labor laws), and governance in general. *The focus should be on implementation* as much as on the passage of laws.
- In the future, the Bank can be better prepared to identify and address rapidly growing poverty by giving high priority to the *monitoring of poverty levels* from the very beginning of its involvement in a country.
- *Greater transparency* can increase public accountability and discourage corruption. The Bank should go out of its way to implement its own disclosure policies and disseminate its analytical work and should encourage governments to report more regularly and fully to their parliaments and to the public at large. The use of *information and communications technology* has tremendous potential to increase public accountability.
- *Economic and sector work* plays an important role through increasing knowledge and training

ESPAÑOL

zación. *La rehabilitación, el socorro de emergencia y los proyectos de importaciones críticas,* que representaban más de la tercera parte de los proyectos energéticos, tropezaron con dificultades debido a problemas de adquisiciones y conflictos entre los objetivos a corto y largo plazo; esos proyectos *deberían diseñarse de manera de reducir al mínimo las demoras (usar listas negativas en lugar de tratar de identificar de antemano las importaciones críticas) y dejar a un lado las unidades de ejecución de proyectos y los objetivos de reforma a largo plazo.* Casi dos tercios de los proyectos de energía se centraron en objetivos a más largo plazo, y los resultados satisfactorios tendieron a ser el corolario de un enfoque programático, con una combinación de operaciones de ajuste e inversión, acompañadas de una labor analítica. Esta fue también una forma eficaz de incluir cuestiones que excedían el ámbito del financiamiento del sector energético, como la eliminación de los subsidios a las entidades del sector de la energía; una mayor disciplina en cuanto a la medición, la facturación y la cobranza; la reforma de las políticas de fijación de precios, y el cierre de las instalaciones antieconómicas de producción de energía. La participación de las partes interesadas demostró ser eficaz en algunos casos, como la privatización de las minas de carbón de Rusia. En otros casos, los progresos fueron limitados. Los esfuerzos por incorporar las preocupaciones ambientales fueron en general eficaces.

En retrospectiva, es probable que se haya puesto demasiado énfasis en la privatización y la reestructuración, y muy poco en la reglamentación, el

FRANÇAIS

et les installations mal entretenues. Les problèmes du côté de l'offre étaient encore aggravés par le manque d'efficacité au plan de la consommation, le fait de ne pas mesurer cette consommation d'énergie et la réticence des usagers à payer. Aucune des dispositions réglementaires ou institutionnelles nécessaires à l'exploitation commerciale n'était en place et il existait de graves problèmes environnementaux.

La politique initiale de la Banque en matière de prêts au secteur de l'énergie électrique consistait à subordonner le financement de la Banque à des réformes dans trois domaines : exploitation du secteur sur une base commerciale, exploitation des entreprises publiques sur un mode commercial et réglementation dans des conditions de pleine concurrence. Dès 1996, la Banque adoptait une démarche privilégiant le dégroupage (« unbundling ») et la privatisation pour faire en sorte que ce secteur fonctionne sur une base commerciale. *Les projets de modernisation, de secours d'urgence et d'importations de produits essentiels,* qui représentaient plus d'un tiers des projets énergétiques, se sont heurtés à des difficultés en raison de problèmes de passation des marchés et de conflits entre objectifs à court terme et à long terme ; de tels projets *devraient être conçus de façon à minimiser les retards (en utilisant des listes négatives plutôt qu'en cherchant à identifier à l'avance les produits essentiels à importer) et renoncer aux unités d'exécution de projets et aux objectifs de réforme à long terme.* Près des deux-tiers des projets énergétiques portaient sur des objectifs à long terme, et les réalisations satisfai-

ENGLISH

local researchers. Its quality in the transition countries has been high, but its impact on the country dialogue could have been greater if it had been more relevant and timely.

• *Aid coordination*, which still needs improvement in many transition countries, can increase the effectiveness of all assistance. Recipient governments should lead aid coordination, with donors helping them define clear development strategies, including monitorable action plans for implementation.

ESPAÑOL

fortalecimiento del desempeño financiero y administrativo de las empresas de servicios públicos, y la lucha contra la corrupción. Como ha señalado la Oficina Regional de Europa y Asia Central, los intentos de convertir entidades estatales no comerciales en empresas privadas comerciales de servicios públicos en general fracasaron, aunque en algunos casos (como en Kazajstán y en algunos países de Europa central y oriental y del Báltico) trajeron aparejadas mejoras en el sector (la reducción de los subsidios, por ejemplo), e incluso en los casos en que el método no tuvo pleno éxito, la calidad y el alcance de los servicios han mostrado una tendencia a mejorar. La incorporación a la UE es un factor de motivación importante para algunos países, pero en muchos otros no era realista esperar que la reestructuración y la privatización permitieran superar los obstáculos jurídicos, políticos, estructurales y de actitudes. *Los objetivos primordiales de las empresas del sector energético deberían ser el mejoramiento del desempeño comercial y la gestión de gobierno de las empresas y del sector. El orden en que deben introducirse las reformas, así como la factibilidad de la privatización inmediata, dependen de las circunstancias de cada país. El Banco debe formular directrices operacionales con respecto a qué secuencia de reformas y medidas funciona mejor en determinadas situaciones nacionales.*

Conclusiones y recomendaciones intersectoriales

Los equipos del Banco que comenzaron a trabajar en países del grupo

FRANÇAIS

santes résultaient plutôt d'une démarche programmatique, alliant opérations d'ajustement et d'investissement et travail analytique. Cette démarche permettait également de traiter de façon efficace des questions qui dépassaient le cadre des prêts au secteur énergétique, notamment les questions ayant trait à l'élimination des subventions aux entités du secteur énergétique ; au renforcement de la discipline en matière de mesure de la consommation, de facturation et de recouvrement des sommes dues par les usagers ; à la réforme des politiques de fixation des prix ; et à la fermeture des installations de production énergétique non-rentables. La participation des parties prenantes s'est révélée efficace dans certains cas, notamment dans celui de la privatisation des mines de charbon en Russie. Dans d'autres cas, les progrès sont restés modestes. Les efforts déployés pour intégrer des préoccupations d'ordre environnemental ont donné de bons résultats dans l'ensemble.

Rétrospectivement, on a probablement accordé une trop grande importance à la privatisation et à la restructuration, au détriment de la réglementation, du renforcement des résultats financiers et des résultats de gestion des entreprises de services publics, et de la lutte contre la corruption. Comme l'a fait observer la Région Europe et Asie centrale, les tentatives de passer d'un système caractérisé par des entreprises d'État ne fonctionnant pas sur un mode commercial, à un système d'entreprises de services publics exploitées selon les lois du marché n'ont généralement pas été couronnées de succès, même si dans certains cas (Kazakhstan et certains

ESPAÑOL

de transición de la región de Europa y Asia central, cuyo conocimiento anterior de esos países era limitado, con frecuencia se vieron obligados a embarcarse en programas de asistencia sin poder darse el lujo de hacer un análisis cuidadoso. En retrospectiva, las conclusiones y recomendaciones del DEO basadas en ese tumultuoso período de cambios económicos, sociales y políticos tienen por objeto contribuir a orientar muchos de los preceptos de política y procedimientos del Banco. Con esta idea en mente, presentamos una serie de conclusiones pertinentes a varios sectores y que permiten formular recomendaciones aplicables en un plazo más amplio no solamente a los países en transición sino también a muchos otros:

- Cuando el Banco comienza a trabajar por primera vez en un país —o después de un largo período de inactividad, cuando se hace necesario actualizar los conocimientos sobre ese país— es aconsejable mantener *el monto de los préstamos dentro de límites prudentes*, hasta que se haya adquirido un mejor conocimiento de la situación y se perciba una mayor *certeza en cuanto a si los programas se sienten como propios.*
- La experiencia en países como Polonia y Rusia (reestructuración del sector del carbón) y Bulgaria (reforma del sistema de pensiones) muestra que, por bien que esté diseñada una reforma, los progresos que ésta logre dependerán en gran parte de que el gobierno se identifique con ella y del grado de consenso que éste

FRANÇAIS

pays d'Europe centrale et orientale ainsi que dans les pays baltes) cette évolution s'est traduite par des améliorations sectorielles (déclin des subventions, par exemple). Toutefois, même lorsque cette démarche n'a pas apporté tous les résultats attendus, la couverture et la qualité des services s'est plutôt améliorée. Pour certains pays, l'entrée dans l'UE est une puissante motivation, mais dans le cas de beaucoup d'autres il n'était pas réaliste de penser que la restructuration et la privatisation permettraient de surmonter les obstacles juridiques, politiques, structurels et de modifier les attitudes. *Les entreprises relevant du secteur énergétique devraient se fixer comme objectifs principaux d'améliorer leurs résultats commerciaux ainsi que la gouvernance des entreprises et du secteur. L'ordre dans lequel doivent se faire les réformes dépend des conditions particulières de chaque pays et la faisabilité d'une privatisation immédiate doit également être déterminée au cas pas cas. La Banque doit mettre au point un cadre opérationnel permettant de déterminer quel est l'ordre de succession des réformes et des interventions le plus adapté aux situations particulières des pays.*

Conclusions et recommandations de portée générale

Les services de la Banque qui ont commencé à travailler sur les pays en transition du groupe Europe et Asie centrale sans avoir, au préalable, de connaissances particulières sur ces pays, ont souvent été amenés à entreprendre des programmes d'aide

ESPAÑOL

pueda movilizar en la sociedad en general. Una sociedad civil bien informada puede convertirse en una importante fuerza impulsora del cambio. Los programas destinados a *hacer tomar conciencia a las partes interesadas y fomentar la participación de éstas* deberían aplicarse en forma más generalizada.

- Las estrategias de asistencia a los países deberían promover el sentido de identificación del gobierno con las reformas y el consenso a favor de éstas, mediante el fortalecimiento de la capacidad de los gobiernos y de la sociedad civil. Estas estrategias deberían incluir un análisis de los procesos políticos, sociales y económicos subyacentes que afectan el comportamiento de las partes interesadas.

- Un marco institucional y regulatorio apropiado y un sector público capaz y transparente son elementos clave de un sector privado orientado al mercado que sea eficiente. *El Banco debe hacer un análisis de la gestión de gobierno y la administración del sector público antes de otorgar préstamos por montos elevados*, en particular cuando es probable que ciertos problemas evidentes afecten los programas de asistencia. La elaboración de estrategias para el cambio institucional y la reforma de la administración del sector público deben encararse con *un criterio amplio y a largo plazo.*

- *La reforma legal y judicial es fundamental* para mejorar el clima comercial (leyes de sociedades, valores, quiebras y antimonopólicas; el respeto de la propiedad

FRANÇAIS

sans pouvoir se permettre le luxe d'une analyse détaillée. Avec le recul, les conclusions et les recommandations que l'OED tire de cette période agitée de changements économiques, sociaux et politiques, ont pour but de contribuer à orienter un grand nombre des principes et procédures de la Banque. En gardant cet élément à l'esprit, nous présentons plusieurs conclusions recoupant divers domaines d'intervention et conduisant à des recommandations applicables de façon très générale non seulement aux pays en transition mais également à bien d'autres pays :

- Lorsque la Banque entame pour la première fois des activités dans un pays — ou lorsqu'elle y reprend ses activités après une longue interruption et qu'une mise à jour des connaissances dont elle dispose à propos de ce pays s'impose — *la plus grande prudence est de rigueur dans l'octroi des prêts aussi longtemps que l'on ne dispose pas de meilleures informations et que l'on n'arrive pas à déterminer avec plus de certitude dans quelle mesure les autorités sont prêtes à prendre en charge les programmes.*

- D'après ce que nous avons pu constater dans des pays comme la Pologne et la Russie (restructuration de l'industrie charbonnière) et en Bulgarie (réforme du régime des retraites), quel que soit le soin apporté à la conception d'une réforme, la réussite de celle-ci est largement tributaire du sentiment d'adhésion des pouvoirs publics et du degré de consensus de l'ensemble de la

ESPAÑOL

privada, los derechos contractuales), el sector financiero (la banca y el banco central, garantías, decisiones relativas a bancos fallidos), los sistemas de protección social (leyes laborales) y la gestión de gobierno en general. *Debería hacerse hincapié en el cumplimiento* de las leyes tanto como en su aprobación.

- En el futuro, el Banco puede estar mejor preparado para detectar rápidamente un aumento de la pobreza y tomar medidas paliativas si asigna alta prioridad a la *vigilancia de los niveles de pobreza* desde el comienzo de su actuación en un país.
- *Una mayor transparencia* puede mejorar la rendición de cuentas en el sector público y desalentar la corrupción. El Banco debería hacer todo lo posible por aplicar plenamente sus propias políticas de libre acceso a la información y difundir su labor analítica, así como alentar a los gobiernos a presentar informes más completos y periódicos a sus parlamentos y al público en general. El uso de la *tecnología de la información y las comunicaciones* tiene un enorme potencial para mejorar la rendición de cuentas en el sector público.
- La labor económica y sectorial desempeña un papel importante como medio de aumentar los conocimientos y capacitar a los investigadores locales. Su calidad en los países en transición ha sido alta, pero su influencia en el diálogo nacional podría haber sido mayor si hubiera sido más pertinente y oportuna.
- *La coordinación de la ayuda,* que aún debe mejorar en muchos

FRANÇAIS

population. Lorsque la société civile est bien informée, elle peut devenir un puissant facteur de changement. Les programmes ayant pour objet de *susciter une prise de conscience de la part des parties prenantes et d'encourager leur participation* devraient être largement reproduits.

- Les stratégies d'aide-pays devraient favoriser la prise en charge des réformes par les autorités et la formation d'un consensus à ce sujet, par le biais d'un *renforcement des capacités* des pouvoirs publics et de la société civile et cela plus particulièrement dans les pays où les réformes n'avancent pas au rythme désiré. Elles devraient intégrer une analyse des processus politiques, sociaux et économiques sous-jacents ayant une incidence sur le comportement des parties prenantes.
- L'existence d'un cadre institutionnel et réglementaire adapté et d'un secteur public compétent et transparent sont des éléments-clés qui déterminent l'existence d'un secteur privé efficace fonctionnant selon les mécanismes du marché. *Un travail analytique sur la gouvernance et la gestion du secteur public doit être effectué avant que la Banque ne décide d'octroyer des prêts importants,* surtout lorsque des problèmes évidents ont de fortes chances d'avoir une incidence sur les programmes d'aide. La mise au point de stratégies visant à introduire des changements institutionnels et une réforme de la gestion du secteur public requiert *l'adoption d'une démarche exhaustive et à long terme.*

ESPAÑOL

países en transición, puede aumentar la eficacia de toda la asistencia. Los gobiernos receptores deberían dirigir la coordinación de la ayuda, con la colaboración de los donantes en cuanto a definir estrategias claras de desarrollo, incluidos planes de acción para la aplicación susceptibles de seguimiento.

FRANÇAIS

- *La réforme du système juridique et judiciaire est d'une importance critique* pour le climat des affaires (droit des entreprises, droit des sûretés, législation relative aux faillites des entreprises et à l'encontre des monopoles ; respect de la propriété privée, droits contractuels), le secteur financier (opérations des établissements bancaires et de la banque centrale, nantissement, faillites bancaires), la protection sociale (droit du travail), et la gouvernance en général. *L'accent doit être placé sur l'exécution de la législation* autant que sur l'adoption des lois.
- À l'avenir, la Banque sera plus à même d'identifier la montée rapide de la pauvreté et de s'y attaquer si elle accorde davantage la priorité au *suivi des niveaux de pauvreté* dès le commencement de ses activités dans un pays.
- *Une plus grande transparence* peut renforcer la responsabilisation du secteur public et décourager la corruption. La Banque ne devrait ménager aucun effort pour mettre en œuvre ses propres politiques de diffusion de l'information et faire connaître son travail d'analyse, et elle devrait encourager les autorités à faire rapport de façon plus régulière et plus complète à leur parlement et au grand public. L'utilisation des *technologies de l'information et des communications* peut jouer un rôle non négligeable dans la responsabilisation des pouvoirs publics.
- *Le travail économique et sectoriel* joue un rôle important puisqu'il permet d'accroître le niveau de connaissances et de former

FRANÇAIS

les chercheurs d'un pays. Dans la mesure où il se rapporte aux pays en transition, ce travail est de haute qualité, mais son impact sur le dialogue avec les pays aurait pu être plus important s'il avait été plus pertinent et qu'il était venu plus à son heure.

- *La coordination de l'aide*, qui doit encore être améliorée dans bien des pays en transition, peut contribuer à renforcer l'efficacité de tout le dispositif d'aide. Les gouvernements bénéficiaires devraient prendre l'initiative d'assurer la coordination de l'aide, les bailleurs de fonds se chargeant de les aider à définir des stratégies de développement claires et notamment des plans d'action dont l'exécution puisse faire l'objet d'un suivi.

ABBREVIATIONS AND ACRONYMS

AAA	Analytical and advisory services
APL	Adjustable Program Loans
BMS	Business Management System (IFC)
CAE	Country Assistance Evaluation
CAS	Country Assistance Strategy
CDF	Comprehensive Development Framework
CEB	Central and Eastern European and Baltic countries
CEE	Central and Eastern Europe
CIS	Commonwealth of Independent States (all countries of the former Soviet Union except the Baltic states)
CSE	Central and South East Europe
DAC	Development Assistance Committee of the OECD
EBRD	European Bank for Reconstruction and Development
ECA	Europe and Central Asia Region
EFSAL	Enterprise and Financial Sector Adjustment Loan
ESMAP	Joint UNDP/World Bank Energy Sector Management Assistance Program
ESW	Economic and sector work
EU	European Union
FDI	Foreign direct investment
FIAS	Foreign Investment Advisory Service
FIL	Financial Intermediary Loan
FSU	Former Soviet Union
GDP	Gross domestic product
GNI	Gross national income
IBRD	International Bank for Reconstruction and Development
IDA	International Development Association
IFC	International Finance Corporation
IFI	International Financial Institution
IMF	International Monetary Fund
LIL	Learning and Innovation Loan
MIGA	Multilateral Investment Guarantee Agency
OECD	Organisation for Economic Co-operation and Development
PPAR	Project Performance Assessment Report
PSAPT	Private Sector Advisory Services in Policy Transactions
PSD	Private Sector Development
PSM	Public Sector Management
QAG	Quality Assurance Group
SAL	Structural Adjustment Loan
SDC	Swiss Agency for Development and Cooperation
SECAL	Sectoral Adjustment Loan
SEE	Southeastern Europe
SOE	State-owned enterprise
SPRITE	Social Policy Reform in Transition Economies
TA	Technical assistance
TATF	Technical Assistance Trust Fund
WBI	World Bank Institute
WDI	World Development Indicators (World Bank)
WDR	World Development Report

Strategy, Implementation, and Outcome

S ince 1989 the transition countries of Europe and Central Asia (ECA) have undertaken massive reforms of their economic systems, transforming institutions, processes, attitudes, and fundamental concepts of individual and organizational behavior.[1] The transition is the subject of a vast literature, and this report does not attempt to summarize what happened. Rather, it has a narrower focus: to use the benefit of 20/20 hindsight to evaluate the World Bank's assistance to 26 countries in the ECA Region[2] in the hopes that the lessons that emerge will prove useful in countries undergoing similar, if less extreme, transitions in the future.

This chapter reviews World Bank assistance to the transition economies and some of the evaluative evidence on its outcome.[3] Five themes were chosen for fuller review, taking into account their relative importance in the Bank's lending program, their relevance to the main goals of transition, and their potential for yielding useful lessons.

Bank Strategy[4]

The Bank's broad strategic objective in the transition countries was to facilitate the transition from a command to a market-based economy through:

- Achieving macroeconomic stability and sound economic management
- Reorienting and strengthening public sector institutions to promote the rule of law, encourage efficient resource allocation, and improve service delivery
- Building the basic institutions of a market economy and an enabling environment for private sector initiatives
- Cushioning the social cost of the transition, especially for the poor and vulnerable.

These objectives were relevant, and to some extent they were included in many of the Country Assistance Strategies (CASs) produced since 1992. (The most common objectives—stabilization and growth; private sector development, or PSD; and social safety nets—each appeared in roughly half of all CASs.) However, the effectiveness of the early strategy was limited for two reasons. First, the initial emphasis on rapid privatization to promote PSD did not always achieve its intended effect because of the lack of a supporting legal and institutional framework. Second, the Bank underestimated the importance of poverty alleviation and good governance. The Region acknowledges that "Poverty was not a central issue . . . a decade ago when [ECA] countries started embarking on the transition from plan to market. The general expectation was that poverty was limited, and . . . very shallow. The presumption was that growth would come quickly [and that] it would reduce the incidence of poverty rapidly. Poverty was believed to be largely transitory in nature, and best addressed through the provision of adequate safety nets" (World Bank 2000c, p. v).[5] Over time the Bank internalized the emerging lessons and shifted its emphasis. The approach to privatization and PSD has evolved considerably. While poverty alleviation was not an explicit CAS objective until 1997, it has become second only to PSD in frequency among objectives in the last five years. Similarly, good governance began to appear as a main CAS objective in 1997.

Implementation

In assessing the effectiveness of Bank assistance, it must be recognized that the collapse of the Soviet Union and the ensuing transition took place with little warning and on an unprecedented scale. The World Bank, like other assistance agencies, faced an enormous challenge at the beginning of the 1990s: to mobilize the resources and knowledge necessary to offer credible support to the new member countries of the ECA Region. Political imperatives put the Bank under pressure to move quickly and lend large amounts, and staff were frequently confronted with the need to act, often under difficult circumstances, in the absence of relevant experience, learning along the way. Country knowledge in the Bank was limited to Hungary, Poland, and Yugoslavia, which were already members.[6]

The Bank geared up rapidly. A new department was organized, financial resources mobilized, and technical and managerial staff recruited. In close collaboration with the International Monetary Fund (IMF) and other institutions, the Bank initiated intensive consultations with the country authorities, most of which had no experience in dealing with these institutions and were undergoing their own internal reorganizations and priority setting. In FY89, the World Bank made three loans to transition countries. Over the next four years, it made 57 loans, mainly to the Central and Eastern European (CEE) countries (figure 1.1). During FY94–98, lending averaged 57 projects yearly, and it peaked at 71 projects in FY99, with the greatest number going to the Commonwealth of Independent States (CIS) of the former Soviet Union (FSU). Since FY00 lending has averaged 44 projects yearly. Lending to some CEE countries has become relatively less important with graduation and accession to the European Union (EU). Since FY89, the Bank has committed over US$42 billion for about 600 projects in the 26 countries under review.

Investment projects comprised four-fifths of the total number of projects and over half of the commitments, although the shares varied significantly by country grouping (figure 1.2). Slightly under half of commitments to Russia and 53 percent of lending to the other CIS countries were for adjustment, while in the CEE and Baltic (CEB) countries, adjustment lending contributed 41 percent of the total.

The greatest single thematic category for lending was economic policy, which received one-quarter of all commitments and ranked second only to the rural sector in numbers of projects (figure 1.3). Seventy percent of all projects were in these two areas plus transportation, social protection, public sector management (PSM), electric power and energy, and finance. As discussed below, many of the projects categorized under "economic policy" include PSM, PSD, financial sector, and energy components.

Technical assistance (TA), both formal and informal, played an important role in Bank assistance. For example, the Bank has had a substantial impact on pension reform policy where it invested administrative or grant resources; loans have rarely been a key part of this process, except to provide financing for the TA. Especially in the smaller countries, focused investment projects with substantial TA often brought stake-

The collapse of the Soviet Union and the ensuing transition took place with little warning and on an unprecedented scale.

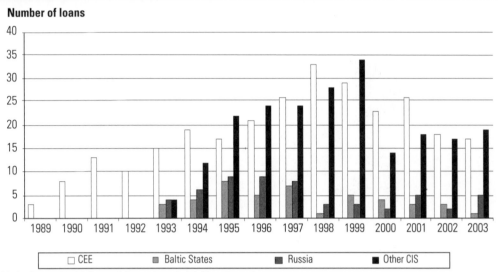

Figure 1.1   **Lending by Subregion, FY89–03**

Number of loans

Source: Annex table A.1. (Annex table A.2 shows which countries are included in each group.)

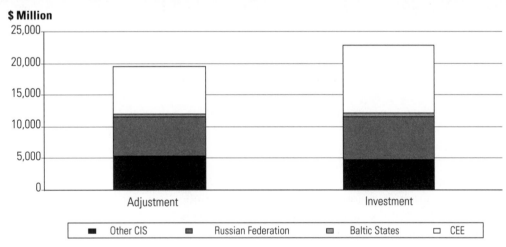

Figure 1.2   **Commitments by Instrument, FY89–03**

$ Million

Source: Annex table A.2.

holders together for the first time and played an important role in preparing for later policy-based lending.[7] Moreover, the simple exposure of local policymakers to staff from the Bank and other donors played an educational role.

In the early years of the transition, while the Bank was building up its assistance, as much as 35 percent of total administrative resources were devoted to analytical and advisory services (AAA). The proportion fell sharply, ranging from 11 to 20 percent during FY95–01, and increased to 27 percent in FY02–03.

Technical assistance, both formal and informal, played an important role in Bank assistance.

Figure 1.3	Commitments and Projects by Sector, FY89–03

Commitments by Sector

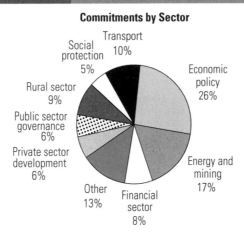

Projects by Sector

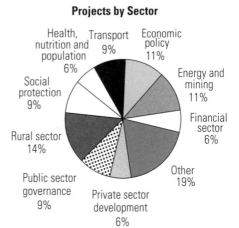

Source: Annex table A.3.

Within the analytical work, some sectors or themes were covered more thoroughly than others. For example, agriculture received relatively high allocations (Heath 2003, p. 7). In contrast, some areas now recognized as critical—poverty analysis, quality of governance, and public expenditure reviews (PERs)—came to the forefront only late in the decade. Although living standards surveys were initiated quite early in a few countries, they tended to focus on short-term labor market and social protection issues; the first poverty assessments were carried out only in the mid-to-late 1990s.[8] A number of Country Assistance Evaluations (CAEs) identify the lack of analytical work and monitoring indicators as an impediment to developing anti-poverty programs.[9] Although billions of dollars were being infused into budgets through quick-disbursing loans (US$5.4 billion to Russia alone), almost no PERs were undertaken in the first half of the decade, and many countries had no public sector analytical work at all until the late 1990s or beyond. Lack of interest by borrowers contributed to this slow pace.[10]

The Bank is one of many actors in the transition countries. In financial flows, the Bank's role was relatively small. Bilateral flows (including the private sector) have

Many countries had no public sector analytical work at all until the late 1990s or beyond.

been by far the most important; EU countries predominate, though less so in the CIS than in the CEB. Multilaterals accounted for only about 16 percent of total net flows in the CIS (14 percent in Russia) and 9 percent in the CEB through 2001. The Bank's share was 5 percent of the total in the CEB and 11 percent in the CIS (figure 1.4). However, the Bank's role was far more significant in terms of analytical work and policy advice. In collaboration with the IMF, the EU, and other donors, the Bank moved quickly to support macroeconomic stabilization and structural reform.[11] In Southeastern Europe, the Bank later mobilized—in conjunction with the EU, the United Nations, and others—to provide post-conflict support. The presence of multiple donors in multiple sectors makes coordination a major task in its own right, and the Bank has sometimes taken the lead in this area. In other countries, particularly those that have become EU members, the Bank has much less influence over the development agenda.

Outcome[12]

As was foreseen, gross domestic product (GDP) fell sharply at the beginning of the transition. In the Central and Eastern European countries, the "transition recession" was relatively shallow and was over fairly quickly; GDP fell on average by less

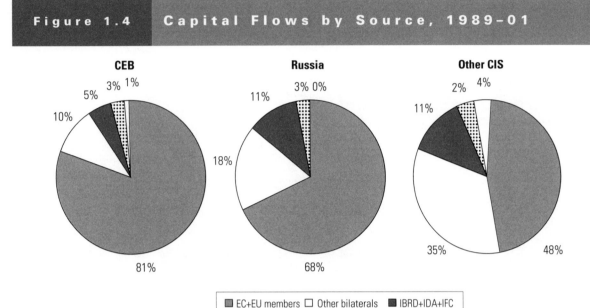

Figure 1.4   Capital Flows by Source, 1989–01

Source: Annex table A.4.

than 15 percent, and per capita incomes recovered in many countries before the end of the decade. The decline in the CIS, however, was far deeper and more prolonged than anyone expected: GDP fell on average by over 40 percent (ranging from 18 to 76 percent), and none of these countries has yet regained its pre-transition per capita GDP, although growth has picked up strongly in recent years (figure 1.5 and annex table A.5).[13] Since 2000, annual GDP growth has averaged over 3.5 percent in the CEB countries, and close to 7 percent in the CIS.[14]

A side-effect of the prolonged transition recession has been the build-up of significant debt problems in some countries that started with very little debt. Official lending levels were based on the expectation that the transition recession would be shallow and of short duration. In a number of CIS countries, where the recession was far deeper and longer than foreseen, and problems of governance more serious than anticipated, this led to significant levels of indebtedness, with effects that are likely to be long-lasting (figure 1.6).

Poverty increased far beyond expectations: at the beginning of the decade, fewer than 4 percent of the population of ECA had to survive on less than US$2.15 per day; by 1998, an estimated 20 percent lived below that level. The incidence of poverty is much greater in the CIS than in the CEB (annex table A.6 and figure 2.4). Inequality, which ranked among the lowest in the world at the beginning of transition, increased as well, more so in the countries with less growth. In some countries—Armenia, Bulgaria, and Russia—the Gini coefficient has nearly doubled (annex table A.6).[15] Infant mortality has dropped in all but two countries, but life expectancy has fallen in most CIS countries (figure 1.7).[16]

The Region made substantial progress in creating market economies: eight countries of the CEB joined the EU this year, and two others are expected to join in the next several years. The European Bank for Reconstruction and Development (EBRD) maintains a set of transition indicators showing progress by country

The decline in the CIS was far deeper and more prolonged than anyone expected: GDP fell on average by over 40 percent.

Poverty increased far beyond expectations.

5

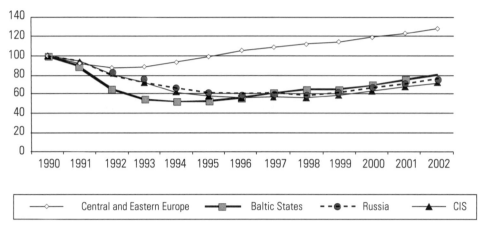

Figure 1.5   **Real GDP Changes, by Group of Countries, 1990–02 (1990 = 100)**

Source: World Bank data.

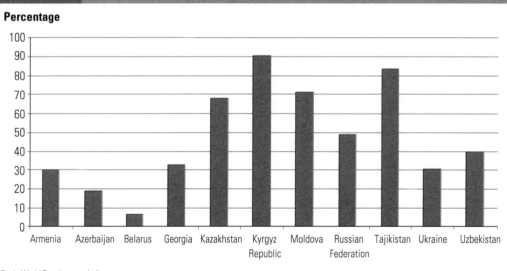

Figure 1.6   **Present Value of Debt as Percentage of GNI, CIS, 2001**

Source: World Bank, World Development Indicators.

With a few exceptions, policy reform has progressed steadily since 1989.

in a number of reform areas (annex table A.7). Scores range from 1, representing little progress, to 4+, which represents standards and performance typical of advanced industrial countries. With a few exceptions, policy reform has progressed steadily since 1989. By 1994, 20 countries (out of 27[17]) had already achieved a 3 (substantial progress) or higher in price liberalization, and 15 had achieved a 3 or more in trade and foreign exchange liberalization (figure 1.8). By 2003, almost all of the remaining countries showed substantial progress in both these areas.[18] This evaluation does not examine these early reforms, or the loans that supported them, except to the extent that they included the thematic areas covered in Chapter 2.

| Figure 1.7 | Change in Life Expectancy at Birth, 1990–01 |

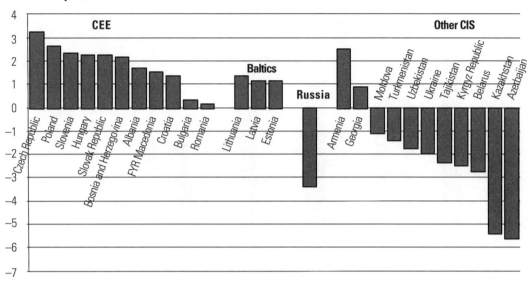

Source: Annex table A.6.

In 1994 only one country had privatized more than 50 percent of large state-owned enterprise and farm assets, and 7 (mostly CEB) had privatized at least 25 percent; 10 (9 of them CEB) had completed small-scale privatization, and another 5 had implemented a nearly comprehensive program. By 2003, 20 had privatized at least 25 percent of large enterprises, and all but 2 had completed or were on the verge of completing small-scale privatization. Nine of the countries (8 of them CEB) had a private sector share of GDP of 50 percent or more in 1994; by 2002, 22 countries derived at least half of their GDP from the private sector, and 11 of them (9 CEB), 70 percent or more. The areas with the least progress were financial sector reform, corporate governance/enterprise restructuring, and competition policy, where only 12, 8, and 5 countries respectively (all but one CEB) had achieved a score of 3 or higher by 2003.

Differences in initial conditions may explain some of the variations in the extent of reform among countries, but the magnitude of their influence is not clear. The EBRD (1999, pp. 27–28) analyzed the impact of initial conditions, using factors such as the degree of industrialization, the ge-

ographical orientation of trade, the extent of initial macroeconomic imbalances, and the legacy of central planning. They found that while initial conditions were important, they were not solely responsible for the pattern of reform. For example, the Baltic countries have achieved substantially greater progress than the western CIS countries, despite similar starting points, and Poland is one of the most advanced countries, although it started in a position very close to Romania. Other pairs of countries that started out with similar conditions but experienced widely different rates of reform include Croatia and Bulgaria, and the Kyrgyz Republic and Uzbekistan. De Melo and others (2001) also concluded that while initial conditions (levels of development and resources, macroeconomic distortions, trade interdependence, location, years under central planning, and so on) helped explain the rate of economic liberalization and growth, economic liberalization was the most important factor determining differences in growth. Political reform was, in turn, the most important de-

By 2003, all but 2 countries had completed or were on the verge of completing small-scale privatization.

Figure 1.8	Number of Countries Achieving Substantial Progress (Rating 3 and Above), 1994–03

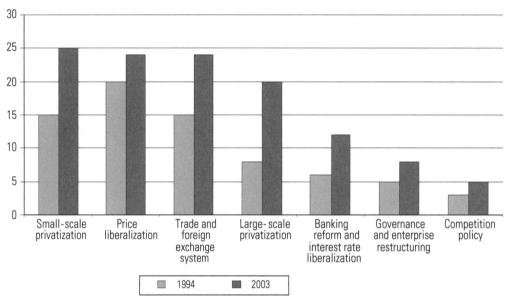

Source: Annex table A.7.

terminant of the speed and comprehensiveness of economic liberalization. Falcetti, Raiser, and Sanfey (2002) found that initial conditions dominated the impact of reforms on growth, and that the positive impact of reforms was less robust than previously thought. They concluded that although the final verdict on the importance of economic liberalization and privatization to growth in the transition was not in, early reforms alone were insufficient to generate sustainable growth.

The areas most frequently identified as warranting greater attention have been PSD, institutions, and public governance and accountability, as well as public awareness and participation, and capacity building for monitoring and evaluation.

OED has produced Country Assistance Evaluations (CAEs) for nine transition countries. Six rate the outcome of the country program satisfactory, at least for the most recent time period examined (Bulgaria, Kazakhstan, Kyrgyz Republic, Lithuania, Poland, and Russia). CAEs rated the outcome of the country programs in Albania, Azerbaijan, and Ukraine, as well as that of the earlier periods in Bulgaria and Russia, unsatisfactory (annex table A.8).[19] This distribution of outcome ratings is lower than that for OED's other CAEs, but the two groups are not necessarily comparable or representative.[20] Institutional development impact was rated high or substantial in only three transition countries (modest in the others), and sustainability was rated likely in five cases, and uncertain in four.

The areas most frequently identified in CAEs as warranting greater attention have been PSD, institutions, and public governance and accountability, as well as public awareness and participation, and capacity building for monitoring and evaluation. Box 1.1 discusses the extent to which lessons from the transition CAEs have been reflected in subsequent CASs for the same countries. In some cases, such as the importance of participatory CAS preparation and the need for greater attention to governance and legal reform, the increased focus in the CASs probably reflects trends in the Bank as much as it does CAE recommendations.[21]

Box 1.1   CAE Lessons and the CAS Record

CAEs call for building ownership of the lending program through higher relevance, sharper prioritization, and greater participation in CAS preparation. Most recent CASs have been prepared with adequate consultations, and they focus on efficiency in discussing portfolio lessons; they generally pay less attention to relevance.

CAEs for the transition countries emphasize the need for core economic and sector work (ESW) (including Poverty Assessments and Public Expenditure Reviews) as a prerequisite for a sound program in any country. The Bank should use the ESW to build local capacity, and disseminate it in the country. Recent CASs emphasize core ESW products; they do not discuss dissemination strategy, nor how these products will be used to help authorities formulate policies and programs. Some large projects still precede relevant ESW.

CASs do not discuss how to encourage increased government management of aid coordination or better monitoring and evaluation. While they often cite the principle of comparative advantage, they rarely use it as an operational guide. Good discussions of comparative advantage can be found for Hungary, Kazakhstan, the Kyrgyz Republic, and Slovenia. Few CASs adequately explore the role of the IMF, nor do they provide the specifics of how the International Finance Corporation (IFC), the Multilateral Investment Guarantee Agency (MIGA), and the Bank will work together.

CAEs have pressed for greater realism in discussing risk, along with improved contingency planning for risky countries. Most CASs have a good discussion of risk to the Bank, but risk mitigation strategy is defined mainly in terms of lending volumes. Many indicators proposed in CASs are couched in qualitative terms and are not monitorable, although the use of monitorable indictors is growing.

As recommended by CAEs, CASs now give substantial attention to governance, and, to a lesser extent, to legal reform. While CASs acknowledge that enforcement of laws and regulations is weak and the judiciary ineffective, the strategy to deal with these issues is not clear, although in the case of infrastructure, CASs do emphasize the regulatory framework. Attention to financial sector issues is generally satisfactory, with the exception of improving financial accountability. There is little discussion of corporate governance issues and remedies.

Regarding other issues raised in the CAEs, CASs have virtually no discussion of which projects or programs will be used to mainstream gender issues and objectives, and rarely discuss decentralization. However, agriculture is receiving greater attention in CASs, which are now addressing the issue of how to respond to the vested interests that dominate the sector in a number of countries.

Source: Annex B.

Project outcomes in the transition countries are rated lower than those for the Bank as a whole by amount of net commitments (74 percent satisfactory, compared with 78 percent Bankwide), but higher by numbers of projects (82 percent satisfactory, compared with 74 percent Bankwide, figure 1.9).[22] Institutional development impact and sustainability rate higher by both measures in transition countries than Bankwide. The bulk of the transition countries fall into the middle-income category. When broken down separately for low- and middle-income countries, the former retain their rankings relative to the Bankwide numbers with respect to outcome—better by number of projects and worse by commitments—but their performance is relatively lower for sustainability and institutional development impact. Outcome ratings for middle-income countries remain below the

Bank average by commitments and about the same by numbers of projects (annex table A.9).

Across the Region, the project ratings are above the Bank average for all of the CEB countries (annex table A.9). There are large variations among the CIS countries, where outcome ratings vary from close to 100 percent satisfactory by commitments (Kazakhstan, Kyrgyz Republic, Ukraine) to 5 percent or less satisfactory (Belarus, Turkmenistan).[23] In Russia, only 40 percent of commitments have been rated satisfactory; high ratings for sustainability reflect the irreversibility of most of the policy and institutional changes.[24] The percentage of active projects rated at risk, by numbers and by commitments, is about the same as the Bank average, but much higher in the CIS than in the CEB (annex table A.10). Ratings by sector are shown in annex tables A.11 and A.12. Although

Figure 1.9   **Project Ratings by Country Group and Bankwide, Approved FY89–03**

Outcome (% satisfactory)

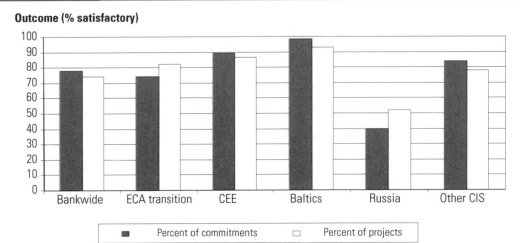

Source: Annex table A.9.

the transition countries have higher rates of satisfactory outcomes than the Bank average in many sectors, in three of the sectors with the greatest amount of lending—economic policy, rural, and transportation, representing 44 percent of commitments—they are substantially lower.[25]

Economic and sector work (ESW), to the extent that it has been done, receives high marks, particularly for quality, both inside the Bank and among clients. The Bank's Quality Assurance Group (QAG) has reported on the quality of ESW since FY98. In all but one of those years, tasks in ECA countries scored above the Bank average in percentage of reports rated at least satisfactory (annex table A.13).[26] All of the tasks sampled in FY01 and FY02 were rated satisfactory. OED's knowledge of the impact of PERs indicates that, in the cases where they *were* carried out, their outcome and impact were higher in ECA than in any other Region. PERs for Latvia (1994), Russia (1995), and Bosnia and Herzegovina (1997, impact not evaluated) were cited as best practice. Borrowers are

Economic and sector work receives high marks, particularly for quality, both inside the Bank and among clients.

CAEs, however, have questioned the adequacy of ESW.

positive about the role of ESW; some point out that knowledge, including ESW and TA, was the Bank's most valuable contribution, and others would have liked more of it (box 1.2).

CAEs, however, have questioned the adequacy of ESW. Eight CAEs found the quality of ESW to be satisfactory, but found its relevance or timeliness unsatisfactory in three countries, and its impact on the country dialogue unsatisfactory in five. The Russia CAE (OED 2002c, p. ix) concluded that "An assistance strategy oriented around analytical and advisory services . . . with limited financial support for Russia would have been more appropriate than one involving large volumes of adjustment lending,"and a project assessment for a series of adjustment and TA loans to Georgia stated that more ESW (particularly an earlier PER) would have helped in designing the reform program.

Bank administrative costs, both per dollar of total commitments and per dollar of commitments with satisfactory outcome or nonrisky status, have been nearly the same on average in the transition countries as in the Bank as a whole, but with large subregional variations. Costs per dollar of commitments were about average for the CEE countries, more than double the average for the Baltic states, about half the average

Box 1.2	**Borrowers' Views of Economic and Sector Work**

Hungary: "The Bank's economic and sector work was of high quality both in terms of the incorporated knowledge and views from within the country and of practical recommendations....[Its] efficacy ... can be seen in its contribution to intellectual debates, particularly in the debates on pension reform and higher education.... The Bank's high level [ESW] has been an indispensable part of its assistance."

Kazakhstan: "ESW was, to a large extent, relevant and helpful to the country's policymakers. It laid the background and framed the thinking for discussions with the World Bank."

Poland: "The impact of the World Bank experts and the [ESW] was assessed as very considerable for the policy dialog in the country and for the capacity building of the government and other elites, especially in the early years ... when the decision makers in the country learned the new, market approach to the economy."

Source: Blaszczyk, Cukrowski, and Siwiñska 2002, p. 5; Báger 2002, pp. 6, 11, 18; Jandosov 2002, p. 12.

for Russia, and about 50 percent above average for the rest of the CIS. After adjusting for the average size of projects, more transition countries had costs per dollar of commitments below what would be expected than above.

Thematic Findings

Chapter 1 presented standard evaluative data on the effectiveness of Bank assistance to the transition economies, but this information alone does not lead to recommendations for improving the Bank's effectiveness. Accordingly, this chapter looks at a few key areas of Bank assistance with a view to identifying lessons.

It summarizes the main findings of five background papers prepared for this study.[1] The five areas—PSD, PSM, financial sector, social protection, and energy—were chosen because of their importance to the Bank's lending program (see figure 1.3) and to the critical issues of transition.[2] A sixth lending category, economic policy, includes a significant number of components and conditions in the five areas. However, the evaluation does not include all areas where the Bank was active. The Bank's experience with price and trade liberalization, where significant achievements were realized and sustained, is not reviewed; the latter is the subject of an ongoing OED study. Two other important sectors—agriculture and health—have been addressed in previous OED studies (see boxes 2.1 and 2.2).[3]

The education sector, which has not been reviewed by OED, and which accounted for less than 3 percent of commitments through FY03, has recently been highlighted in a Regional strategy paper (World Bank 2003). That paper found that although, at the start of the transition, both the Bank and the countries thought that edu-

cation was not a problem sector, a much more sobering picture has emerged. The curricula, textbooks, and teaching practices do not support acquisition of the skills necessary for market economies and open societies; inequities in learning opportunities are growing; the gross enrollment rate in basic education has fallen in many countries (annex table A.6); most countries have significant inefficiencies; the sector is still dominated by government, inadequately counterbalanced by competition and participation; and severe limits on public budgets compound the problems, with energy and wage bills crowding out other inputs, and a severe infrastructure crisis in the CIS. Systematic monitoring of the situation could have revealed these problems sooner.

The five selected thematic areas are interrelated. For example, PSD in the transition countries is as fundamentally about restructuring institutions that deal with fiscal expenditure, welfare provision, regulation, monitoring, and adjudication as it is about promoting the growth of the private sector. A poorly clarified division of

Box 2.1	Reforming Agricultural Policy in Transition Economies

The Bank has provided substantial support to the reform of agricultural policies, including high-quality analytic work. Rural lending in the transition economies is second only to multisector projects in the number of projects financed (figure 1.3), and more than half of all Bank agriculture sector reviews in the early 1990s were devoted to these countries. Rural projects as a whole have lower rates of satisfactorily rated outcomes than either the average for ECA or rural projects Bankwide, but results vary significantly across themes. Trade liberalization is largely complete, and considerable advances have been made with land reform and in developing rural financial markets, but less has been accomplished in post-privatization follow-up and the reform of state institutions serving the sector. Land policy and rural finance, which have received more Bank resources than have other areas, are also associated with the best project results. There is evidence of a moderately positive relationship between the level of agriculture policy reform and agriculture productivity growth. Despite the greater attention to rural poverty in recent strategy statements from the ECA Region, there is no evidence yet of improved project monitoring of living standard indicators. Nor is there much discussion of poverty in project documents.

OED's study found no evidence that particular instruments of Bank assistance were more effective than others, emphasizing the need to tackle policy reform with a battery of complementary instruments, including analytic work, technical assistance, adjustment lending, and investment lending. Experience suggests that institutional and land reform should have been addressed at the beginning of the transition. Some small pilot projects achieved major results; for example, most state and collective farms in Azerbaijan have been privatized, based on a pilot project financed by the Bank.

Source: Heath 2003.

Box 2.2	Supporting a Healthy Transition: Evidence from Selected Countries

Health reform is a difficult, long-term process involving a wide range of stakeholders, and it is further complicated by the absence of a widely agreed model for the financing and structure of health systems. The Bank's financial contribution is typically small relative to total health financing in a country, so its influence depends on catalyzing wider reforms. The outcomes of reforms have varied considerably: some countries achieved improvements in system performance and outcomes (Estonia); others face continued deterioration in health services and stagnation in health indicators (Romania).

The Bank's initial health projects in the Region underestimated the political and institutional difficulties of reforms, and were thus over-optimistic regarding the pace and prospects for reform. There is remarkably little evidence on the impact of reforms, reflecting the lack of priority given to monitoring and evaluation. The Bank's most successful projects, and its most significant contributions to the sector reform process, resulted from lending or nonlending support for building capacity and consensus for reform. Given regular turnover of governments and ministers, engagement with a wide range of stakeholders, including Parliament and opposition parties, is essential. Projects were also more likely to be successful when carried out in partnership with other donors, nongovernmental organizations, or research institutes. The impact of studies and analyses depended on the extent of local involvement and dissemination (Albania, Hungary, Romania) and on the government's absorptive capacity for technical analysis (Albania, Romania). The Bank can further enhance its contribution to sector reform through improved monitoring and evaluation at the project and sector levels and through continuing to experiment with new lending instruments, including Adjustable Program Loans and Learning and Innovation Loans.

Source: Johnston 2002.

fiscal responsibilities between branches and levels of government created an unstable business environment. The limited capacity of tax administrations led to tax evasion and arrears, unevenly applied tax rules, and a gap between effective and statutory rates, driving entrepreneurs into the informal sector. The competitiveness of existing enterprises was undercut by their energy inefficiency (spurred by past state energy subsidies) and by their social safety net responsibilities. The financial impact on the enterprises of collapsing markets, economic pricing of energy, and continuing social expenditures was cushioned by continued subsidies through the banking system and from the energy companies. The failure of governments to develop sustainable, financially sound welfare systems has made these governments loath to sever ties with enterprises, and has encouraged them to support loss-making enterprises that provide significant non-wage benefits to employees. These issues and others will be taken up in the remainder of this section. Chapter 3 will discuss some crosscutting lessons and recommendations.

Private Sector Development[4]

A major goal of the transition was to transform state-dominated and controlled economies into market-driven, private sector–oriented economies through the privatization of state assets, the imposition of market discipline on state-owned enterprises (SOEs), and encouragement of new private enterprises.[5] Both borrowing governments and the Bank quickly identified PSD as a central reform priority. Loans to Poland and Russia in 1991–92 helped shape a Bank strategy for PSD assistance with enterprise reform at its core. The central objective was to establish a critical mass of profit-seeking corporations, no longer dependent on state support for their survival, and a class of owners willing to invest in their enterprises and manage their restructuring. More recently, post-privatization restructuring and assistance programs have grown in importance. Other categories of Bank assistance that con-

Private property has become the dominant basis for productive transactions in most of the transition economies.

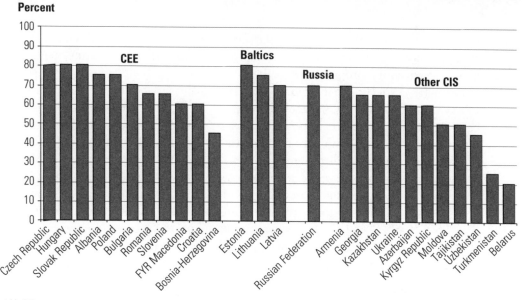

Figure 2.1   Private Sector Share of GDP, 2002

Source: Annex table A.7.

Box 2.3　　IFC's Support to Transition Economies

IFC's country assistance strategies focused on privatization assistance (including advisory work); pre- and post-privatization finance; development of financial markets; assistance to small and medium-size enterprises (SMEs); and investments in infrastructure and export-oriented industries generating foreign exchange. IFC broadly succeeded in following these strategies. Approval volumes were constrained mainly by external factors such as the absence of necessary reforms or interested sponsors, the Russian crisis, and the EBRD's substantial market presence.

IFC strategies emphasized non-investment operations as a way to leverage IFC's expertise for maximum impact, initially in the FSU countries (where viable investment opportunities were limited by the dearth of suitable local companies having an acceptable sponsorship or ownership structure and by the macroeconomic downturn), and later also in Central and Southern Europe as IFC increased its selectivity in that region. This strategy led to unprecedented volumes of technical assistance (TA), totaling US$170 million and including US$55 million in trust fund (TATF) assignments and US$12 million in PSAPT assignments, or one-third of TATF and PSAPT approvals worldwide, in FY90–03. The Foreign Investment Advisory Service (FIAS) performed 104 diagnostic reviews and other assignments, one-fifth of its global work.

Within its investment operations, during FY90–03 IFC approved a net US$5.9 billion, or 14 percent of its worldwide net approvals for the period, in 432 transition country projects, with particularly high volumes in Russia (US$1.7 billion); Czech Republic and Kazakhstan (US$0.5 billion each); and Hungary, Poland, and Romania (US$0.4 billion each). In line with strategic priorities, approvals were concentrated in finance (27 percent), infrastructure (17 percent), and oil and gas (10 percent). IFC also mobilized US$2.2 billion in syndicated loans from commercial banks.

A comparison of 61 mature investment projects in transition countries with 317 evaluated projects in other countries shows that transition country projects had similar development outcome success rates and similar IFC work quality ratings, but significantly lower investment outcome success rates, and thus a significantly lower proportion of projects with both satisfactory-or-better development and investment (win-win) outcomes. This is not a surprising result given the pioneering nature of IFC's operations in the Region—they were likely to produce substantial development impacts, but exposed IFC to a greater degree of investment risk. Outcomes in Central and South East Europe (CSE) and the Baltics were somewhat better than those in the FSU. Projects in strategically targeted sectors and areas yielded mixed results:

- **Privatization-related projects** had lower development and investment outcome success rates than other projects, reflecting problems related to the sustained "old-style" management of privatized companies.

---

tained PSD components include financial sector strengthening, regulatory and judicial reform, and compensatory programs for vulnerable groups (all discussed later in this report). The contributions of IFC and of MIGA are summarized in boxes 2.3 and 2.4 and annex tables A.14 and A.15. IFC provided substantial amounts of technical assistance in addition to its investments.

Private property has become the dominant basis for productive transactions in most of the transition economies (figure 2.1), but privatization alone could not create a receptive investment climate. Privatization led to better outcomes in the advanced reformers of the CEB than in the CIS countries. In the more advanced reformers, firms have made significant progress in cutting ties to the state, resolving financial difficulties, attracting investment, developing new products, and finding new export markets. The entry of large numbers of new firms is responsible for much of the job creation in these countries. By contrast, the countries lagging behind have yet to establish favorable conditions for firm-level reforms. Initial reforms have not created the foundations for renewed growth, and significant parts of the enterprise sector in several countries remain in a low-investment, low-restructuring trap.

Bank lending for PSD has had a number of effects. It appears to have had the greatest impact on private sector growth in the CIS, where countries receiving high levels of PSD commitments

The countries lagging behind have yet to establish favorable conditions for firm-level reforms.

- **Financial markets** projects had similar development outcome success rates, but significantly lower investment outcome success rates, than those in the rest of IFC, reflecting the impact of the Russian financial crisis and the slower-than-expected pace of banking system development in most countries.

- **SME** projects, which IFC supported mainly through financial intermediaries, had higher development outcome success rates than similar projects elsewhere. Projects in CSE countries, where entrepreneurial culture was more developed, outperformed non-SME CSE projects on both development and investment outcome, while those in the FSU out-performed non-SME FSU projects on development outcome, but had similar investment outcome success rates.

IFC's transition country investment portfolio has performed very poorly, making a significantly negative net contribution to IFC's income for the FY90–03 period.

While comprehensive evaluation data are not available, TA was delivered in a satisfactory manner and largely yielded positive impacts. On both an ex-ante and ex-post basis, the Operations Evaluation Group (OEG) concludes that the TA-intensive strategy was appropriate, particularly for FSU countries, as an efficacious and efficient way of contributing unique additionality with pioneering reach, achieving broad development outcomes while minimizing investment losses.

The EBRD operates only in transition countries where it has a broader mandate that includes public sector operations. Even excluding the public sector, EBRD's commitments have exceeded IFC's nearly fivefold in CEE countries, nearly fourfold in the FSU, and threefold in the Baltics, and its non-investment support has exceeded IFC's fivefold. EBRD's appetite for investing significant amounts sometimes precluded IFC from attractive investment opportunities, but, overall, its presence alleviated the pressure on IFC to commit larger volumes and enabled IFC to be more selective, albeit within a much-reduced pipeline of opportunities. Because the EBRD has played a major role in the Region's transition for the benefit of PSD in general, it is indeterminate whether its presence had a net positive or negative impact on IFC's investment and development results.

Among the lessons from IFC's experience in transition economies are the need to (1) tailor the mix of investment and non-investment instruments to country circumstances and IFC's learning curve; (2) analyze not only the client's nominal shareholder structure, but also its underlying ownership; and (3) be prepared to intervene with the government to ease regulatory barriers and protect the emerging private sector from unfair practices.

Source: Operations Evaluation Group, IFC.

Box 2.4	MIGA Operations in Transition Economies

During FY90–02, MIGA issued guarantees supporting 88 projects in 20 countries, for a maximum aggregate liability of over US$2 billion (annex table A.15). These guarantees facilitated more than US$5 billion in foreign direct investment (FDI). Four countries accounted for two-thirds of the FDI: Russia alone received 27 percent; Bulgaria, 19 percent; and the Czech Republic and Poland, 10 percent each. Close to half of the guarantees were for financial services, and another quarter for manufacturing, 11 percent for infrastructure, and 9 percent for mining. MIGA also provides information for potential investors through its Investment Promotion Network Web site (IPAnet) and other country-specific sites, such as PrivatizationLink Russia, launched in October 2000.

MIGA's guarantee program in Russia prudently and selectively met demands from private investors for political risk insurance and has suffered no losses. Similarly, in Bulgaria, MIGA did not suffer any claim losses during the 1996–97 economic crisis. However, MIGA did not realize its potential in Bulgaria and Kazakhstan. Bank staff, government officials, and the investment community are not always familiar with MIGA guarantee and technical services, and MIGA could do more within the countries to promote its activities and increase its cooperation with other development institutions, including IFC.

Source: Operations Evaluation Unit, MIGA.

quintupled the size of their private sectors relative to GDP during 1992–00, while countries receiving low levels of assistance only tripled the relative size of their private sectors.[6] In the CEE countries, the Bank had less apparent impact: the relative size of the private sector doubled regardless of the level of PSD assistance. A possible explanation is that foreign direct investment was relatively more important in these countries (see figure 1.4). While revenue generation was not a central objective of privatization, the sale of large SOEs did generate significant proceeds, as high as 20–30 percent of GDP (in Georgia, Hungary, Kazakhstan). More important, PSD assistance appears to have had a substantial positive impact on enterprise reform, although the causality could run the other way, with credible signals from governments regarding reform prompting greater amounts of lending.[7]

The most successful projects for SOE reform and restructuring tended to be either the first major loans to countries, with borrowers who were highly committed to reform (Hungary and Kazakhstan), or loans following major TA or adjustment efforts that laid the groundwork (Armenia, Latvia). The least successful projects generally suffered from powerful domestic opposition, usually from trade unions (for example, in Bulgaria, Poland, and Romania); internal opposition within the governments; or overly ambitious targets based in part on overestimation of borrower capacity and commitment.

Privatization of small enterprises was generally rapid and successful (see figure 1.8). However, the speed and methods used for the privatization of medium-size and large SOEs—and the role of the World Bank therein—have been the subject of major international debate since the beginning of the transition. This evaluation does not attempt to determine who was right and who was wrong, or whether alternative methods might have led to better outcomes. Rather, it presents some of the lessons that can be gained from looking back at the experience.

Privatization of small enterprises was generally rapid and successful. However, the speed and methods used for the privatization of medium-size and large SOEs—and the role of the World Bank therein—have been the subject of major international debate.

Critics have argued that the Bank (along with other donors) gave inadequate attention to institutional deficiencies in the rush to promote the divestiture of medium-size and large SOEs—particularly through sale mechanisms such as vouchers that did not ensure adequately concentrated ownership—and that the Bank devoted insufficient attention to regulatory regimes to strengthen post-privatization ownership structures, corporate governance, and enterprise performance.[8] Reviews of the literature and of internal Bank documents show that reformers and their advisors recognized the need to reform regulatory, anti-monopoly, commercial, capital market, and bankruptcy regimes, but that these were often regarded as "second-generation" reform issues, to be pursued once there was a critical mass of privatized firms. Bank assistance programs initially reflected the view that privatization must take place quickly, taking advantage of limited reform "windows," to prevent the possibility of reversals, including the return of the communists, and that new private owners would restructure the enterprises, provide adequate corporate governance, and lobby for further liberalizing reforms and supporting institutions.[9]

An analysis of CAS objectives shows that in the Baltics, Bosnia and Herzegovina, Kazakhstan, the Kyrgyz Republic, Moldova, Tajikistan, and Ukraine, institutional reform objectives were included before or alongside privatization objectives, and a number of the early lending programs did include projects to support institution building, in addition to privatization and enterprise reform. However, for 17 other countries, institutional objectives appeared late in the decade or not at all. An examination of project documents reveals that very few of the early Bank PSD projects contained specific "institutional" components, and the majority of regulatory reform and competition policy projects were initiated *after* privatization in most transition countries, especially in the CIS.[10]

It should be noted that borrowers often preferred reform packages that emphasized enterprise reforms (especially privatization) at the expense of institutional efforts, and in several cases where "institution building" loans were made *before* enterprise reforms or privatization had progressed substantially (Armenia, Bulgaria, and Ukraine in 1993, Georgia in 1995), the outcomes of these loans were unsatisfactory, mainly because of weak borrower commitment. Where significant attention has been devoted to post-privatization regulatory structures and institutional frameworks to support markets, results are mixed: while many of the laws and institutions supporting markets are now in place in most transition countries, the capacity of a number of governments to enforce them has been severely weakened by frequent changes in regulations, their discretionary interpretation by public officials, and the resulting corruption.

The ownership structure emerging from voucher privatization schemes has been associated with low investment and little restructuring (Djankov and Murrell 2000). In some countries—particularly those for which EU accession was a central policy objective—the requirements of accession prompted the pursuit of second-generation reforms. But in many CIS countries this momentum did not materialize. It soon became evident in some countries that vested interests had become powerful enough to oppose the adoption of institutional and regulatory frameworks that would constrain their further acquisition of wealth. *With the knowledge afforded by hindsight, it is apparent that the Bank, along with other donors, should have tried harder to promote the improvement of the institutional framework for business and investment, as well as, and in parallel with, privatization.*

All transition countries have enterprises whose sale and restructuring has proven highly problematic. In the worst cases, these ailing firms have continued to drain public resources and have bottled up valuable assets that could be used by new firms. In many cases, it was evident early on that the enterprises were value subtracting and would receive little new investment. Reliance on bankruptcy procedures—no matter how well designed—in addition to burdening the limited capacity of the judicial systems, proved disappointing, even in some advanced reformers. Administrative or other out-of-court procedures were often overwhelmed by the enormity of the task, the shortage of staff and institutional capacity, and social or political pressures. *The approach to problematic firms could be improved in the future through greater attention to the design of rule-based administrative procedures to initiate the liquidation of enterprises while they are on the state's balance sheets.*

The emphasis in future privatization should, when circumstances permit, be on more measured, better prepared transactions and on helping governments ensure that the process is transparent, competitive, and open to foreign participation. The lagging reformers often have little knowledge of trade sales, workouts and liquidation, or investor-led restructuring. For internal political reasons, government officials are frequently reluctant to use outside experts. *The Bank and IFC/EBRD should work in tandem, with the Bank helping to organize the process, and the IFC/EBRD making investments.*[11]

The bulk of PSD assistance until the late 1990s was devoted to the privatization of existing SOEs, rather than support for new firms. Experience demonstrates, however, that in both advanced and slow reformers, recovery was achieved largely because of the the expansion of new firms. *The Bank is now focusing more heavily on promoting improvements in the business environment, with an emphasis on removing barriers to the entry of new firms and barriers to exit for others, and creating incentives that allow existing firms to move out of the informal sector (World Bank 2002b). A variety of legal reforms are needed—in company law, collateral laws, security laws, bank-*

> *While many of the laws and institutions supporting markets are now in place in most transition countries, the capacity of a number of governments to enforce them has been severely weakened by frequent changes in regulations, their discretionary interpretation by public officials, and the resulting corruption.*

> *Future privatization should ensure that the process is transparent, competitive, and open to foreign participation.*

Political analysis could have informed the Bank's work to a greater extent than it did.

ruptcy and anti-monopoly laws. Moreover, *respect for private property and contractual rights and the assurance that judicial enforcement is competent and non-corrupt will remain critical for the growth and expansion of the private sector.*

Finally, political analysis could have informed the Bank's work to a greater extent than it did. For example, staff communications regarding Poland's privatization program reveal a fear of enterprise workers' councils, particularly when it came to granting them a veto over the privatization of their firms. In the event, widespread protests against reform by workers did not, for the most part, materialize. There were strikes and demonstrations against enterprise reforms—particularly among coal miners in Ukraine, Romania, and elsewhere—but these were relatively localized. More often, workers—and labor unions—emerged as allies of enterprise reform. In Poland and the Czech Republic, for example, it was the labor unions that served as a check on the excesses of SOE managers (limiting their asset-stripping and theft) and that demanded second-generation regulatory and institutional reforms following privatization. This finding suggests that *greater emphasis should be placed on building local constituencies—not merely entrepreneurs, but workers and reform-minded local politicians as well—capable of demanding further policy reforms.* These constituencies can be developed through consultations with civic groups—particularly those representing labor interests and business associations.

The Bank's ECA Region carried out its own study of the transition after 10 years (World Bank 2002b). The lessons and agenda for the future that emerge from that study are reproduced in box 2.5. OED agrees with these lessons. With the benefit of hindsight, OED also considers that the Bank should have pursued this agenda sooner than it did.[12] In the earliest years of the transition, many of the

At the start of the transition, few in the Bank were focused on assistance for governance and PSM reform.

choices made by the Bank were probably appropriate, given what was known at the time. However, by the mid-1990s, it is reasonable to ask whether the Bank was focusing sufficiently on the climate for PSD and the appropriate methods for privatizing medium-size and large enterprises.[13]

Governance, Public Sector Management, and Institution Building[14]

At the start of the transition, few in the Bank were focused on assistance for governance and PSM reform. The *World Development Report 1983: Management in Development* had highlighted the role of good government in development, and the Bank's first PSM team had been established in the early 1980s within central projects staff, but from the late 1980s through the mid-1990s, the subject received little attention. The ECA Region established a small group in the early 1990s, but did not build up a substantial number of specialists until 1997 (the year in which the *World Development Report* focused on the role of the state). The Bank's approach to governance was first set out in a 1992 publication entitled *Governance and Development*, which recognized that the quality of governance had a determining impact on economic development and was therefore an appropriate matter for the Bank to address (see also Shihata 1991).

A review of transition CASs in the early to mid-1990s shows little concern with governance, a finding not unique to the ECA Region. During the period FY94–98, the proportion of lending Bankwide for public sector governance was 8 percent, and for rule of law, 1 percent. In ECA, lending for these areas was 9 percent and 2 percent of the total respectively; only the Latin America and Caribbean Region lent as high a share of its resources to these areas. Nonetheless, in retrospect, the modest efforts—by the Bank; by other donors; and, most important, by the countries themselves—to address the countries' weak capacity to manage the reform process were not sufficient in the face of the persistence of poor governance, a high degree of "state capture" by private interests, and pervasive bureaucratic corruption.

The first Bank report to discuss corruption openly appeared in 1997 (World Bank 1997b). In

Box 2.5

**Lessons from *Transition*—
The First Ten Years**

- Privatization should be part of an overall strategy of discipline and encouragement.
- Small enterprises under state ownership (generally enterprises with fewer than 50 employees) should be sold quickly and directly to new owners through an open and competitive auction, without restrictions on who may bid for the shares.
- Medium-size and large enterprises should target sales to strategic outside investors. With a concentrated, controlling interest, they will have a clear stake to best use the enterprises' assets. Although several transaction methods may be used, including negotiated sales, this can be brought about most effectively through competitive "case-by-case" methods, more deliberative than voucher schemes or rapid, small auctions. They use independent financial advisors who both prepare the enterprise for sale and act as sales agents on behalf of the state.
- Investor protection should be enshrined in the legal system and enforced, covering rules to protect minority shareholders; rules against insider dealings and conflicts of interest; creditor surveillance accounting, auditing, and disclosure standards; and takeover, insolvency, and collateral legislation. When court enforcement of contracts is weak, these provisions should be supplemented by a stock market regulation for financial intermediaries, such as investment funds and brokers, who then have an incentive to ensure compliance by other participants in financial markets. This will set the stage

for privatization of future medium-size and large enterprises. It will also improve the performance of existing privatized enterprises by assisting transparent consolidation of shares where ownership is diffuse. It will also facilitate bank- and nonblank-based financial intermediation.
- Privatization should be accompanied by increasing competition in the market for the products sold by the enterprise in question and vigorously enforced by the competition policy authority. This can discipline managers in an environment where corporate governance is weak.
- The cash flow and property rights of the state should be clarified for enterprises in which the state continues to hold an ownership stake.
- [a] Divesting enterprises in sectors characterized by natural monopoly or oligopoly (where average production costs decline continuously as scale increases and the market and society are best served by one or a few enterprises) must proceed with great caution, if at all. Advances in technology have made such sectors increasingly rare. But where they exist—as in local distribution of natural gas—an efficient regulatory regime that protects the public interest is a prerequisite, lest divestiture transform an inefficient public monopoly into a poorly regulated or nonregulated private monopoly.

Source: World Bank 2002b pp. 79–80.

2000 the ECA Region published *Anticorruption in Transition.* In the same year the Bank issued its first major strategy paper on public sector reform (World Bank 2000d), which confirmed that governance had become a central concern of the Bank. Almost all transition CASs now place PSM reform at the center of the assistance strategy, and this has been reflected in recent projects. An example of this turnaround is Albania: the CAE found that the lack of focus on governance and institutional reform was a critical omission during 1992–97. Since 1999, however, OED project assessments have found that the Bank has made a substantial contribution to PSM reform, including the introduction of a medium-term expenditure framework and initiation of ju-

dicial and public administration reform. Similarly, in Russia the Bank largely neglected PSM at first—neither of the first two quick-disbursing loans (1993 and 1995) included PSM reform—but since 1998, it has supported significant public sector reforms. Assistance to the Kyrgyz Republic through 2000 included only one project and no ESW addressing governance and PSM; the most recent projects take a comprehensive approach, using adjustment and TA and covering a wide set of interrelated issues, including civil service reform, accountability, and civil society voice and access.

Almost all transition CASs now place PSM reform at the center of the assistance strategy.

Stakeholder analysis should be standard practice, and an integral part of program and project design.

Given the many influences at work, it is difficult to distinguish the impact of Bank assistance from that of other participants. At least some of the available data suggest an improvement in governance over the past six years. The World Bank Institute's (WBI) governance database includes indicators of governance performance across 6 dimensions for 27 transition economies. Ninety-five observations showed improvement between 1996 and 2002, while 65 recorded deterioration.[15] Progress was uneven across the dimensions: "regulatory quality" showed the greatest improvement (18 countries), while "control of corruption" showed the least (11 countries). "Voice and accountability," "political stability," and "rule of law" each improved in about 16 countries. The CEB countries, particularly those acceding to the EU, have made greater progress than the others (figure 2.2). In 2002, the lowest scores for the CIS countries were generally in "control of corruption" and "voice and accountability," while the lowest scores for the CEB countries (though still above the CIS) were in "control of corruption," "rule of law," and "government effectiveness." Further evidence is found in the Bank's reports on corruption in ECA (World Bank 2000a; 2004), which show mixed but generally encouraging trends in both the CEB and CIS.[16] However, concerns over data comparability put these conclusions in doubt, and other sources of data—for example, the Global Competitiveness Survey—indicate that corruption in ECA is increasing, not decreasing.

It appears that an inadequate understanding of the political and social situation contributed to failures in some operations, such as when the Ukraine Parliament rejected a loan that had already been negotiated.[17] *The design and implementation of reform initiatives should be based on an understanding of the underlying political and social processes at the core of government that determine the motivation and behavior of stakeholders.* Such understanding would enable the reforms to take into account the realities that help

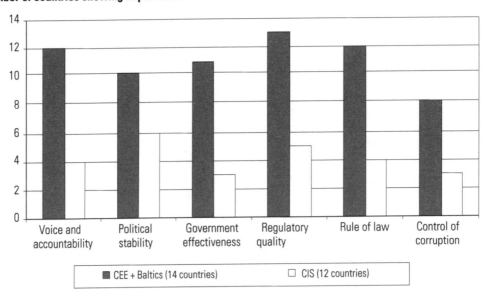

Figure 2.2 **Improvements in Governance Indicators, 1996–02**

Number of countries showing improvement

Note: Total sample, 26 countries: Bosnia and Herzegovina not included in government effectiveness and control of corruption measures.

Source: WBI Governance Indicators (http://www.worldbank.org/wbi/governance/govdata2002).

explain the functioning of public institutions.[18] Stakeholder analysis, which until recently was largely absent from the ECA Region's work programs, should be standard practice, and an integral part of program and project design. The Region has recognized the importance of this work in recent publications (World Bank 2002b) and seminars; boxes 2.7 and 3.1 provide good examples from a number of countries.

Many of the components of a PSM reform strategy are interdependent, with financial, legal, administrative, and personnel aspects. They also cut across sectors. Yet in most of the cases examined for this study, reform was approached in an *ad hoc*, incomplete manner, without a comprehensive, cross-sectoral institutional development and PSM reform strategy. Moreover, institutional reform goes beyond changing organizational structures and rules; it also involves discarding long-established habits and patterns of behavior—a complicated and lengthy process. Major institutional changes of the kind needed in the transition economies may have to be spread over several decades, rather than compressed within the time frame of one or a few adjustment loans. Two relatively new instruments—Adjustable Program Loans (APLs), with their ten-year horizon, and Learning and Innovation Loans (LILs), designed to support reforms involving a long learning process—seem to be well suited to the situation in some transition economies. A Bank review of the early experience with such lending noted that it was particularly suitable for dealing with institutional reforms involving substantial changes in bureaucratic behavior. Where it is relevant, *the ECA Region should seek to adopt a long-term strategy for institution building assistance, based on a "learning approach," with a 10–20 year commitment*, with the understanding that programs will need to be modified over time.[19]

Public expenditure analysis has long been a central focus of Bank economic work, but, as noted above, it received little attention in the transition economies until the late 1990s. In the meantime, the Bank had transferred considerable sums to transition economies (especially Russia) in the form of adjustment loans, without the benefit of credible systems of public financial accountability, detailed knowledge of inter- and intra-sectoral expenditure allocations, or information on the distortions from budget execution, which may deviate substantially from budget allocations. Toward the end of the decade, the pioneering work by the ECA Region, and the surveys by the Bank, the EBRD, and others, documented pervasive corruption and massive diversion of public resources in the Region and opened this area to wide public debate.[20] This work highlighted the importance of confronting corruption, an issue that had previously been taboo for the Bank, as well as the need to link public expenditure analysis with the broader issues of public financial accountability (Sahgal and Chakrapani 2000). In 2000 it become mandatory for country teams to prepare a Country Financial Accountability Assessment, a Country Procurement Assessment Report, and a Public Expenditure Review for each borrower. To date, all three have been completed for only nine transition countries, although the ECA Region is planning to complete these diagnostic studies for all of its countries by the end of FY04. *Given the pervasive corruption so well documented in* Anticorruption in Transition, *this work is clearly of great importance*. OED's recent review of progress in mainstreaming anti-corruption activities in Bank assistance (OED forthcoming) concluded that *the Bank should set minimum governance prerequisites for lending, and this is particularly important when large amounts of money are at stake*.

Improving public financial accountability depends on the willingness of the political leaders and key officials to change the system. One way to build ownership of the reforms is to *have the key players participate in and share the diagnostic*. Most studies to date have not been joint exercises, and it is not clear whether borrowers are truly eager to achieve genuine public financial accountability. Strengthening of public financial accountability generally results in some "losers"; stakeholder analysis can help those pro-

Institutional reform involves discarding long-established habits and patterns of behavior—a complicated and lengthy process.

The governments should prepare time-bound, monitorable action plans, agreed with the donor community.

moting reform to understand and modify the incentives facing key actors to motivate them to support reform. Following the studies, *the governments should prepare time-bound, monitorable action plans, agreed with the donor community.*

A key tool to increase public accountability and discourage corruption of all types is transparency. The Bank has had a major influence through its insistence in projects on transparent practices in areas such as procurement and tax administration.[21] While recognizing that increasing attention is being paid to promoting a culture of transparency, more emphasis is warranted. The ECA Region should go out of its way to make all its studies and documents public and to disseminate them fully— the Bank already has a disclosure policy that is very supportive of this objective, but the delivery is still weak.[22] In addition, through all its operations, *the Region could encourage governments to report more regularly and more fully to their parliaments and to the public at large* (through government

Most transition economies urgently need assistance for judicial reform.

Web sites). Equally, the Region could encourage all governments to replace their secrecy laws with public information acts along the lines now being proposed in Uzbekistan.[23]

E-governance, the use of information and communications technology, *has tremendous unexploited potential to increase public accountability* by improving the transparency of government actions, tracking the movement of funds, and reducing the number of face-to-face interactions between the officials and the public where corruption might arise (in paying customs duties and taxes, obtaining permits, registering land, tendering and procurement, and the like). The ECA Region has only a pilot project in this area. Box 2.6 presents some examples of the benefits of e-governance in another Region.

Establishing the rule of law is critical if the transition economies are to build successful democratic market-based economic systems. Most transition economies urgently need assistance for judicial reform, an important aspect of the rule of law, but the ECA Region, along with the rest of the Bank, geared up slowly in this area. No CASs discussed judicial reform before FY97, and in the following four years, only three cited problems in the judiciary, although many identified deficiencies in specific laws. Through 2001, the

---

Box 2.6 **Reducing Corruption through E-Government in India**

The Department of Revenue in Karnataka has computerized 20 million records of land ownership by 6.7 million farmers in the state. Previously, farmers had to seek out the village accountant to get a copy of the Record of Rights, Tenancy and Crops (RTC), a document needed for many tasks such as obtaining bank loans. There were delays and harassment. Bribes had to be paid. Today, for a fee of Rs.15, a printed copy of the RTC can be obtained online at computerized land record kiosks in 140 offices.

The Central Vigilance Commission has begun to share with citizens a large amount of information related to corruption. Its Web site has published the names of officers from the elite administrative and revenue services against whom investigations have been ordered or penalties imposed for corruption. Through

the use of computers and other electronic devices at 10 remote interstate border check posts in Gujarat, India, a team of public officials has reduced corruption and significantly increased the state's road tax revenue.

The Vijaywada Online Information Center (VOICE) delivers municipal services such as building approvals and birth and death certificates, and handles the collection of property, water, and sewerage taxes. The VOICE system uses five kiosks located close to the citizens. It has reduced corruption, made access to services more convenient, and improved the finances of the municipal government.

Source: http://www1.worldbank.org/publicsector/egov/india.htm

Region had supported only six stand-alone judicial reform projects. While another 11 had significant judicial reform components, and 79 had legal reform components, these often supported passage of laws or supplied equipment, rather than encouraging the reform of systems. Moreover, three-quarters of these projects came only after FY95. Evaluation reports suggest that the majority of laws supported by the Bank have been submitted or passed, but that legal reform has not yet met the broader objectives stated in the loan documents (Gupta, Kleinfeld, and Salinas 2002). This is a big issue for EU accession countries. *While the focus on this important area has increased, additional attention is warranted, possibly including the creation of judicial reform capacity within the ECA Region.*[24]

Governments are unlikely to carry through a major reform of PSM unless pushed and monitored by a vocal, informed, and organized civil society. *A well-conceived strategy for public sector reform will include initiatives to mobilize and build the capacity of civil society*, including NGOs, civic organizations, professional associations, business chambers, and the press—the "drivers for change." The Bank largely ignored civil society in this context, but *some innovative initiatives have taken place during the last three years (box 2.7); they should be greatly expanded in the future*.

Financial Sector[25]

At the outset, transition economies possessed financial systems whose basic purpose was to allocate funds according to the plan, with a limited capacity to intermediate financial resources and no need for prudential regulations of financial supervision. Initial CASs, with few exceptions, treated financial sector reform as a central element of the transition. The immediate objectives were to create an efficient and unified payments and settlement system; the policies, institutions, and instruments necessary to design and execute monetary policy operating through market processes; and an efficient system for mobilizing savings and directing them toward the most promising investors and investments, bringing market discipline to bear on the decisions and management of the borrowers themselves. In broad terms, the assistance programs have been highly relevant. A basic understanding quickly formed in the Bank with respect to the essential elements of financial sector transition, and these elements were repeated in almost all the countries where active programs and dialogues were sustained. Macroeconomic stability was emphasized as a precondition for healthy financial development. Bank programs focused on putting in place the basic legal and regulatory framework and accounting systems for a market-based financial system, with initial emphasis on the banking sector. Efforts were made to impose market discipline on the decisions of banks and enterprises through hard budget constraints. However, such constraints were not always enforced. Moreover, the need to reform the enterprise and banking sectors in parallel was

> *A well-conceived strategy for public sector reform will include initiatives to mobilize and build the capacity of civil society.*

Box 2.7   Ukraine—Strengthening Civil Society

A "People's Voice" project, promoted by the Bank, aims to build integrity in municipal government and pressure local leaders from below to improve public service delivery. Surveys have been used to provide monitoring and feedback. This has led, for example, to the establishment of one-stop citizen service centers. One municipality established working groups to respond to the service weaknesses revealed by the surveys. The 2000 CAS, recognizing that governance and institutional reform would only be successful if there was true ownership by government, Parliament, and a majority of civil society, stated that the Bank will work "in partnership with stakeholders and will incorporate benchmarks of increased transparency and accountability in its operations."

sometimes ignored, and the magnitude of the required shift in social expenditures away from enterprises was underestimated.

The Bank's financial sector analytical work has generally been of high quality, but its timing may have reduced its impact: fewer than one-third of the reports reviewed for this evaluation were completed in the first half of the decade (through 1996), but during this time more than half of the lending operations with financial sector components were approved. Some extreme cases were Armenia, Georgia, and the Kyrgyz Republic, where the first pieces of formal financial sector work appeared only in 1999–00, following substantial Bank lending in the financial sector, and Albania, Bosnia and Herzegovina, and Poland, where no dedicated formal financial sector work was found at all, despite numerous loans aimed at least partly at financial sector objectives.[26]

The number and volume of Bank loans for financial sector development rose rapidly after 1991. Lending began to taper off after 1996, reflecting progress in some cases, frustration in others, and a tendency of the EU accession countries to rely increasingly on European assistance. Both governments and external donors often responded to rapidly unfolding events with stop-gap measures, and lending programs and policy dialogues were interrupted by changing governments or by policy reversals. Country circumstances varied widely. Thus, although specific reform elements are common to most programs, it is not surprising that the Bank did not follow a common approach to the selection or sequencing of operations. For example, in a few cases (such as the 1995 assistance strategy for the former Yugoslav Republic of Macedonia), staff asserted that Bank credit line operations would require the satisfactory implementation of banking reforms under the ongoing adjustment loan. In other cases, staff argued that credit

Both governments and external donors often responded to rapidly unfolding events with stop-gap measures, and lending programs and policy dialogues were interrupted by changing governments or by policy reversals.

was essential for spurring a supply response from the private sector and could not wait until the macroeconomic and sectoral policy and institutional framework were perfected (Albania and Bosnia and Herzegovina). In a few cases, lending programs comprised only one or two operations over the entire decade, either because of lack of agreement on strategy (Belarus, Slovak Republic, Turkmenistan) or lack of interest in borrowing (Czech Republic).

The Bank's assistance to financial sector transition cannot be evaluated by adding up or averaging the programs undertaken in 26 different countries. At the extremes, a very modest Bank intervention in Estonia was associated with highly positive results because of foreign investment and the reform dynamic and skills already available in the country (annex table A.7 includes some indicators of financial sector reform). Limited interventions in Belarus and Turkmenistan, in contrast, were associated with virtually no progress at all, which was explained largely by the countries' resistance to change. Among countries ranked as top performers by the end of the decade, Hungary and Poland each benefited from substantial financial sector lending programs.[27] However, after a very large lending program with financial sector objectives, Russia was still in the lower echelon of countries in financial sector development. The size of the programs responded to the degree of interest of governments in borrowing, the rate of progress in implementation, and the degree of external pressure on the Bank to keep resources flowing. In addition to differences in initial conditions, results depended largely on the ability and willingness of governments to reform institutions and make the difficult political decisions required.

Most transition economies have made tangible progress toward the development of market-based financial systems. Figure 2.3 shows, for example, growth in credit to the private sector. However, levels of financial development varied widely by the end of the decade, with the CEB countries significantly more advanced than those of the CIS.[28] Major issues remain to varying degrees in all countries, including inadequate financial sector supervision and accounting

| Figure 2.3 | Change in Domestic Credit to Private Sector, 1993/95 to 2002 |

Percent of GDP

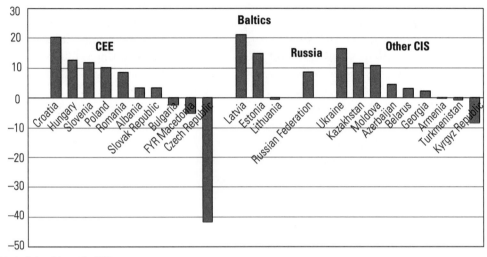

Note: Data for Turkmenistan are for 2000.

Source: World Development Indicators.

standards, poor corporate governance, low levels of monetization and intermediation, small and illiquid capital markets, and weak bankruptcy laws and protection of creditor rights. Efforts to tighten budget constraints on banks and enterprises were largely unsuccessful because of weak administrations and legal institutions, inadequate information, and the heavy social and political costs of enforcement. A number of lessons have emerged.

The constitution of a proper legal and regulatory framework is essential for an efficient market-based financial sector, and Bank programs have correctly emphasized putting this framework in place. However, submitting and even enacting laws is not enough. Some of the laws that were enacted were hastily drafted, and later had to be modified or replaced. *The key is* implementation *of the legal framework, including laws governing banking and central banking, bankruptcy, and collateral.* Slow progress in upgrading the authority and effectiveness of the bank supervisory agency, including the resolution of failed banks, has been a consistent predictor of poor financial sector performance. *Increasing effectiveness of bank*

supervision should be an important trigger for financial assistance. Similarly, while most Bank assistance for financial sector transition has pressed for their adoption, *progress in the effective enforcement of international accounting standards should be viewed as an early indicator of the authorities' determination to carry out reform and as another trigger for Bank financial assistance.*

The most serious shortcomings in the Bank's support to legal and regulatory reform were in underestimating the time and the additional assistance and human resource development required to make the new laws and regulations effective. The virtual absence of specialized lawyers, judges, accountants, and other professionals was recognized and given considerable emphasis in the Bank's policy papers and ESW reports, and highly specific training was provided through TA and investment loans to the

The most serious shortcomings were in underestimating the time and the additional assistance and human resource development required to make the new laws and regulations effective.

staff of project implementation units, to financial intermediaries participating in Bank credit lines, and to the restructuring and privatization agencies. However, few resources were devoted to the extended training needed to operate the larger system. *High priority should be given to the intensive training of bank supervisors, lawyers and judges, accountants and auditors, and the other skilled professionals on whom the effectiveness of the legal and supervisory framework depends. As noted above, growing recognition in the Bank of the time required for the institutional changes needed to sustain structural change has led to the introduction of new lending instruments, such as APLs, designed to provide continuing support over a longer time horizon.*

Strong, financially sustainable banking institutions are essential to the development of stable financial systems and to the efficient intermediation of financial resources. State-owned banks, especially those emerging from the central planning tradition, have seldom demonstrated long-term prospects for becoming sound and efficient financial intermediaries, and early efforts should be made to attract reputable private strategic investors. Among 17 transition countries to which the Bank lent for privatization, the public share of assets in banks fell from 94 percent in the early 1990s to 20 percent a decade later; this compares to a decline from 77 percent to 25 percent in a worldwide sample of countries. In cases where privatization is not rapid or complete, however, state-owned banks cannot be ignored. *While fully commercialized behavior may be an overly optimistic expectation, substantial efforts are still needed to improve the incentive framework that guides the behavior of state-owned banks, through stronger governance, tighter budget constraints, enforcement of prudential regulations, divestiture of branches, and restrictions on the scope of banking licenses.*

Support to the development of sound financial and regulatory institutions requires a multi-year commitment and is highly supervision-intensive.

Although the Bank was a leader in analyzing the interrelationships between banking sector and enterprise reform and in developing comprehensive programs for reforming the two in parallel, some of the major analyses and assistance efforts did not take them into account. In Russia the early, rapid privatization of both banks and enterprises apparently obscured the continuing interlocking ownership and accompanying governance issues that undercut the reliance on private operators to realize the real sector restructuring and credit reallocations. Country strategies did not pay sufficient attention to how the process could be subverted by the perverse incentives of bank and enterprise managers and interlocking owners. Privately owned banks strongly interlinked with major borrowing enterprises make poor candidates for sound and efficient intermediation. *Measures are needed early in the transition process to strictly enforce prudential regulations, which can include minimum capital requirements and limiting loan concentration and related-party lending. Bank ownership and governance issues should, along with financial viability, be scrutinized carefully in determining the eligibility of financial institutions to participate in Bank TA programs and credit line operations.*

Institutional development programs for participating banks should attach high priority to strengthening basic banking skills, such as credit policies and procedures, risk management, internal controls and information systems, including accounting standards. Support to the development of sound financial and regulatory institutions requires a multi-year commitment and is highly supervision-intensive. The Bank and other donors have provided large amounts of TA for this purpose. Even when other donors finance the assistance in the context of a broader Bank program, the Bank should monitor its progress, since it is crucial to the success of the overarching objectives. Assessment of this progress should be a central consideration in the decision of whether to go forward with a follow-up project.

Close to half of all operations with financial sector components in the transition economies over the past decade have included lines of credit intermediated through private or public financial institutions, although total commitments for such projects have fallen dramatically. Over three-quarters of the Financial Intermediary Loans (FILs) in the ECA Region have been in sectors other than finance, with the biggest concentration in the rural sector. The wide variation found in the timing, design, implementation, and evaluation of FILs suggests a continued widespread ambivalence within the Bank about their proper objectives, including the financial sustainability of the intermediaries, and the conditions under which they should be carried out. Moreover, the underlying assumption that credit would be a binding constraint on PSD in the early transition experience can be questioned in hindsight, as the utilization of credit lines was far less than anticipated: 40 percent of commitments approved during FY93–02 were canceled. Ratings of projects containing lines of credit have been particularly low in the financial, rural, social protection, and PSD sectors (less than half of commitments satisfactory). *Financial sector staff should be systematically involved in the design of financial intermediary operations and should ensure that the factors that will determine the sustainability of the financial flows, instruments, and institutions being supported are adequately taken into account.* [29]

As the number of FILs has fallen, a growing share of recent operations has supported the start-up of rural and microfinance institutions, which initially depend on government and/or donor resources. Their eventual sustainability and independence will require a capacity to mobilize savings and attract commercial funds. *Microfinance projects should give greater attention to developing savings services and the resulting supervision requirements, and they should include a donor exit strategy from the start.*

Capital markets development was sometimes overemphasized in the early years of the transition, both within and outside the Bank, as a principal means to rationalize corporate governance and finance enterprise restructuring, and the attention given this issue was counterproductive to the extent that it drew attention away from more immediate concerns. No formal stock market could have played the role assigned to it by the mass privatization proponents without first having a properly functioning banking system, adequate accounting and auditing conditions with effective disclosure requirements, responsible corporate governance, and protections for minority shareholders, and the problem was exacerbated by most shares being in the hands of individuals with little idea of their meaning and worth. While *the development of efficient capital markets* is an important component of financial sector development, it *does not have the same urgency as the need to build a strong banking system.*

Social Protection[30]

The transition strategy adopted by the donor community gave high priority to stabilization of the economy and structural reforms to modernize and privatize key economic sectors. Reform of the social protection system was viewed largely as a way to cushion the impact of the disruptions from the structural reforms.[31] But the transition presented major challenges for social protection systems. The changes in industrial structure increased, at least in the short run, the demand for assistance to job losers. Lower-income households needed protection from consumer price increases resulting from the removal of indirect subsidies, and assistance programs required more effective targeting as unemployment rose and compensation differentials increased. Privatization of enterprises that had formerly maintained records and paid most social protection benefits required the creation or reform of government or other specialized institutions to administer benefits. Finally, all of these changes took place at a time of diminished fiscal capacity. Pension programs were particularly affected. With privatization and increased self-employment, often up to half of the labor force fell out of the formal system, sharply reducing contributions, while most of those already eligible, along with new retirees, still qualified for benefits based on previous employment. It also became clear that new forms of intergovernmental fiscal arrangements were needed to allow national and local governments to share the fiscal burden.

The Bank had had little experience with so-

Often up to half of the labor force fell out of the formal system.

cial protection programs. Its initial social protection reform agenda for the transition economies emerged from sector reviews undertaken in the early 1990s on several countries, and was articulated most completely in *Labor Markets and Social Policy in Central and Eastern Europe* (Barr 1994). Bank activities generally followed this agenda, and subsequent internal analyses confirmed its relevance.[32] Areas of primary emphasis included strengthening employment services, reforming pension systems, and improving benefits targeting. The agenda for pension reform, particularly the recommended move to flat benefits, was not popular in many transition countries.

The situation was complicated by an alternative model, presented in *Averting the Old Age Crisis* (World Bank 1994), based primarily on experience in Latin America and focused exclusively on pension reform, where it advocated a three-pillar system.[33] This model was not inconsistent with the long-run agenda in *Labor Markets* (Barr 1994)—the first pillar would provide the minimum income guarantee of the flat benefit structure—but if adopted too early in the transition, its shift to advance funding for the second pillar (comprising individual accounts) would exacerbate the fiscal problems of transition governments by diverting some of the pension contributions being used to finance payments to current retirees. It also ignored first-pillar sustainability problems, especially evident in transition countries with their mature demographic structures. Moreover, its implementation required the creation of fairly sophisticated financial and regulatory institutions.

Lending focused initially on helping employment services deal with the expected surge of displaced and unemployed workers.[34] Although rated satisfactory, these early projects, like those in other sectors, suffered from instability in the government institutions and inexperience of the borrowers in dealing with Bank projects. Most important, job dis-

> *By mid-decade, the pension programs of most transition countries had become major fiscal problems, while deteriorating economies were causing sharp increases in poverty rates.*

placements proved far fewer than anticipated in the short term, particularly in the CIS countries, and where unemployment rates *had* risen, the slow growth of alternative employment opportunities undermined retraining efforts. Moreover, the governments and the Bank had not anticipated the longer-term unemployment problem—people too old to be retrained who could not realistically find new jobs. The result was large expenditures for programs not originally designed to deal with this problem, such as pensions for early retirement or disability.

By mid-decade, financial difficulties in the pension programs of most transition countries had become major fiscal problems, while deteriorating economies were causing sharp increases in poverty rates, particularly in the CIS, exposing the weaknesses in existing social assistance programs (figure 2.4). The Bank's emphasis shifted to pension reform, supporting major changes to the structure of the benefit formula; increases in the retirement age; and the introduction of mandatory, funded pillars in several cases. Twenty countries enacted at least one major reform, usually with significant assistance from the Bank.

The pension reform aspects of a number of the early adjustment loans failed, even when the loans as a whole were rated satisfactory. Later loans, including two to Latvia for a funded second pillar, were more successful.[35] *The Bank has had a major impact on pension policy reform efforts in Bulgaria, Croatia, Estonia, Hungary, Latvia, Lithuania, Poland, and Romania. In many cases the main impact came about through substantial TA*—often in cooperation with other donors—for seminars, interaction with local analysts, and other methods to transfer knowledge to local officials.[36] The TA frequently was associated with lending, and, in some cases, loans helped focus the borrowers' attention on the need for reform, even if the reforms did not occur in the time frame envisioned (for example, Russia in 1997); in others they followed the adoption of the reform and facilitated its implementation (Croatia in 2002).

All the pension reforms followed, at least in part, the model developed for transition countries, and about half incorporated features from

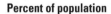

| Figure 2.4 | Poverty Headcount Index ($2.15/day), Latest Year, 1995–99 |

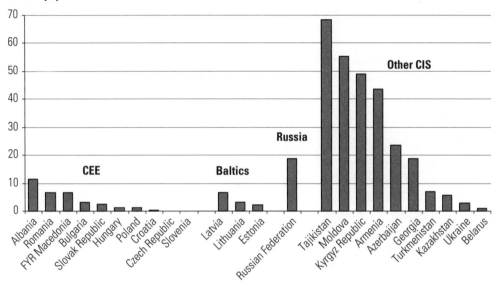

Source: Annex table A.6.

Averting, whose system of individual, funded accounts was attractive to reformers (box 2.8). *Averting* broadened the debate about pension reform and helped secure a place for it on the policy agenda of most countries, but its controversial approach led to major disagreements among international agencies active in assisting pension reforms, as well as within the Bank, and its publication probably delayed pension reforms in some countries (such as Russia). Implementing the approach has been difficult, and

many Bank staff now believe that it is probably beyond the institutional capacity of the less developed of the transition countries (see, for example, Lindeman, Rutkowski, and Sluchynskyy 2000). *A clear strategic approach to pension reform, one that differentiates according to the capacity—both institutional and fiscal—of the country, has been needed for years, and still is.*

The Bank did not devote the same kind of resources or energy to social assistance reform as it did to pension reform. Although the Bank's

| Box 2.8 | Hungary—Promoting Public Debate on Pension Reform |

The World Bank's monograph, *Averting the Old Age Crisis*, generated wide public debate over the issue of pension reform. An unprecedented professional and public dialogue emerged on the introduction of the three-pillar pension system. There was no previous example of such a vivid discussion of policy issues among government experts, stakeholders, and individuals in Hungary. The government and the Parliament finally passed the three-pillar pension system bill in the fall of 1997, and it became effective as of January 1, 1998.

Source: Báger 2002, p. 11.

portfolio of social assistance–related activities is larger than that of pension activities, and most of the project outcomes (or implementation progress) have been rated satisfactory, the successes in the former are far more modest.[37] Conditions attached to adjustment loans were successful in supporting program expansions (for example, Romania), the clearing of arrears (Albania and Tajikistan), or improvements in targeting (Armenia, Bulgaria, and Russia). They were less successful in implementing new programs, as illustrated by the failure in the Ukraine and the cancellation of the last tranche of the Bulgarian Social Protection Adjustment Loan. Many of the activities involved building local capacity to conduct and analyze household surveys (Belarus, Bulgaria, Latvia, and Romania). Even there, TA offered outside of the loan process appears to have been more effective than the lending itself.[38]

ESW has devoted considerable attention to analyzing safety net issues and, starting in the mid-1990s, poverty. Most Bank poverty and social safety net assessments, along with a number of CAEs, conclude that improvements are needed in the size and structure of assistance programs: too great a share of benefits goes to higher-income households; inhabitants of poorer regions of a country find it more difficult to qualify for benefits and receive less; and benefit levels are too low to be of much use in fighting poverty. *If poverty reduction is to remain a major goal in the transition countries, the Bank will have to devote as much attention to the reform of social assistance programs in the future as it has to pension programs in the past.*

Lending tended to neglect administrative reforms, often because the borrowers did not want to pay for technical assistance. Only a small number of the (relatively few) investment loans in the pension and social assistance areas aimed at strengthening the basic institutions responsible for collecting so-

> *Too great a share of benefits goes to higher-income households; inhabitants of poorer regions of a country find it more difficult to qualify for benefits and receive less; and benefit levels are too low to be of much use in fighting poverty.*

cial insurance contributions and delivering benefits. Most pension administration loans dealt with relatively modest administrative improvements, with some notable exceptions, such as a loan to Bulgaria in which TA funded through grants from other donors strengthened the capacity of the social security administration and helped achieve a national consensus on changes not previously acceptable to the public or the Parliament. Half of the loans related to pension administration supported the development of second-pillar institutions, rather than improvements in the operations of the basic system. ESW and the many Bank-sponsored seminars focused almost exclusively on the policy issues associated with pension reform, and virtually ignored administrative issues.

Most transition countries still lack adequate capacity to monitor and analyze their social protection needs and to develop appropriate policy responses.[39] The Bank supported actuarial training in Bulgaria, Macedonia, and Russia. Bank staff worked closely with local analysts on the Polish and Hungarian pension reforms; this assistance focused on the preparation of reforms, with fewer resources to help with implementation. The World Bank Institute (WBI) managed a Training Program on Social Policy Reform in Transition Economies (SPRITE) supported by bilateral donors during 1994–01. An evaluation carried out for WBI (World Bank 2001) found that in the 12 CIS countries it covered, the program helped build a consensus on health and pension reforms, improved technical skills of local specialists, provided continuity to the reform process, created a network of trainers, contributed to collaboration among a variety of institutions, and provided materials that were adopted by academic institutions. However, the program itself was not sustainable when its funding ended, as it did not provide for full cost recovery. A review of recent CASs found virtually no discussion of strategies to further build domestic capacity for carrying out either analysis or projects. Where Bank-assisted reforms have been successful, it is usually only after an extended period of time, during which Bank staff and consultants interacted repeatedly with local reformers, helping them understand and develop their reform options and form a consensus in favor of reform among local leaders. *Adequate resources for these participatory activities are one key to successful social protection reforms; assistance with implementation is also important. The Bank should devote additional attention to building institutional capacity in policy analysis and administration of both pensions and social assistance.*[40]

The contributors to *Labor Markets and Social Policy* (Barr 1994) anticipated the problems many transition economies would have in improving targeting because of their large informal sectors and inadequate information systems. However, until recently the Bank *did far too little to help develop techniques to improve targeting of social assistance benefits*. The case of Armenia shows what can be accomplished: in the late 1990s, the Bank supported integrated living standards surveys. Together with adjustment lending, these surveys facilitated the introduction of a single, targeted poverty benefit, replacing a complex system of child allowances and other benefits that went to poor and nonpoor alike. In addition, highly subsidized rates for electricity, transport, and communal services were substantially eliminated, and replaced with cash transfers to a more narrowly defined group of highly vulnerable beneficiaries. Elsewhere, the Bank held a conference on alternative targeting approaches, sponsored at least one report (Grootaert and Braithwaite 1998), and supported three pilots in Russia. Far more is needed.

While the results of Bank activities in the transition economies generally confirm the relevance of the strategy described in *Labor Markets and Social Policy*, in retrospect, the strategy *should have addressed additional areas that have proven to be barriers to social protection reform in virtually every transition economy*: labor laws that encourage labor hoarding among declining firms and discourage hiring among expanding firms; strategies for sharing fiscal and policy burdens associated with operating assistance programs among levels of government; and special problems in coverage and administration caused by the growth of informal sectors.[41] The strategy should also have recognized

more prominently the regional differences, particularly the differences in institutional capacity, among transition countries.

Social protection systems consist of large, complex, and politically sensitive programs. Fundamental changes in these systems that reduce or eliminate promised benefits are major political challenges. They require extended public discussion and political consensus building, and adjustment loans have proven to be poor mechanisms for helping this process. Adjustment loans are more likely to be effective in encouraging policy change when it involves modest but affordable expansions or when it reflects an existing consensus about the need for and nature of the reform—for example, incorporating an adequate minimum pension provision in Kazakhstan and increasing the minimum pension in Russia in 1997.[42] Investment needs in social protection tend to be rather modest, and clients are reluctant to borrow for TA. Even the ESW sponsored by the Bank will have only limited impact without adequate funds to finance dissemination and discussion of its results. *Thus traditional instruments have not been well suited to reforming social protection systems.*

The weakest link in the Bank's strategy of social protection reform for the transition economies was in translating the larger vision into systematic and strategic agendas at the country level. Only two countries, Russia and Bulgaria, had ESW that attempted to focus broadly on this area.[43] Almost without exception, the social protection sections of CASs were little more than listings of projects in the pipeline.[44] They rarely provided any appreciation of the link between social protection reform and public sector administrative re-

The Bank should devote additional attention to building institutional capacity in policy analysis and administration of both pensions and social assistance.

The weakest link in the Bank's strategy of social protection reform for the transition economies was in translating the larger vision into systematic and strategic agendas at the country level.

form, or sequencing of projects to make sure that the administrative and policy aspects were synchronized. There have been some notable reform successes, particularly in the pension area, but also a number of missed opportunities, particularly in social assistance. The failures appear to be linked to insufficient attention to the development of a policy consensus within the client countries, to improving administrative and other institutional capacities and linking them to the policy development process, and to developing new and innovative ways to target benefits. Countries need a broad public understanding of the reasons for and the nature of the reforms and reform prescriptions, closely tailored to their particular situation. *Social protection reform works best when analytical work, consensus building activities, and institutional capacity building precede the enactment of legislation.*

Energy[45]

The transition countries inherited substantial infrastructure and, in some cases, possessed significant quantities of oil, natural gas, and coal. Traditionally, these sectors were vertically integrated public monopolies, a structure that led to serious inefficiencies in investment, operations, and pricing. Most companies and service providers were heavily subsidized, while customer service was inadequate and facilities were poorly maintained. Supply-side problems were exacerbated by low efficiency of consumption, lack of metering, and unwillingness to pay. None of the regulatory or institutional arrangements necessary for commercial operations was in place, and there were serious environmental problems. Moreover, the sector is particularly prone to corruption because the stakes are high, and the opportunities for rent-seeking, plentiful.

The Bank did not have a great deal of experience in this area (OED, OEG, and OEU 2003a). By the beginning of the 1990s, many Bank staff had concluded that "business-as-usual" lending to public power utilities was un-

Power sectors in most transition countries had little prospect of reaching commercial standards because of the inefficiencies of state ownership and poor governance.

tenable and—after a lengthy process of discussion and debate both within the Bank and between the Bank and outside stakeholders—the Bank issued a policy paper in 1993 on electric power lending (World Bank 1993). The policy (also supported by IFC and MIGA) linked Bank support to country commitment to reforms in three areas: commercialization, corporatization, and arm's-length regulation. This approach called for commercialization and corporatization prior to privatization, as a means to introduce competition, but it did not include strategic or operational guidelines for implementation.

Power sectors in most transition countries had little prospect of reaching commercial standards because of the inefficiencies of state ownership and poor governance, and by 1996, the Bank had in practice adopted a reform approach that also included unbundling and primarily advocated privatization as a means to achieve commercialization. Formally adopted in 1998, this strategy had four main objectives (Lovei 1998; World Bank 1998): (i) protecting the public interest through improved regulatory regimes, demonopolization, increased safety, less environmental impact, and transformation of the sector from a net user to a net provider of budgetary resources; (ii) rehabilitating energy supply facilities, assisting with the institutional aspects of restructuring and privatization, and mitigating the social impact of restructuring; (iii) facilitating private investment; and (iv) promoting regional initiatives to increase energy trade and sharing of information.

An analysis of over 100 completed projects confirms that these long-term objectives were an integral part or even the main objective in nearly two-thirds of them. The rest, primarily for rehabilitation, usually contained institution building or some reform conditionality. In less than one-quarter of the rehabilitation operations did the long-term objectives appear to play no significant part. In retrospect, probably too much emphasis fell on privatization and restructuring, and too little on regulation, strengthening utility financial and managerial performance, and combating corruption.[46] While projects pursued restructuring objectives in 22 out of 24 countries, they dealt with regulation in only 10.

Nonlending instruments focused mainly on policy advice, through freestanding sector reports or notes; training (both formal and on-the-job); and technical assistance, such as that provided by the Joint UNDP/World Bank Energy Sector Management Assistance Program (ESMAP). The strategy also emphasized improved cooperation with external partners and building stakeholder participation.

The outcome ratings of the completed dedicated energy projects are about the same as the average for all projects in the ECA transition countries and higher than the Bankwide average for the sector (annex tables A.11 and A.12). Short-term objectives were achieved through quick-disbursing rehabilitation and emergency recovery projects. The satisfactory achievement of long-term objectives appears to have resulted from a programmatic approach in 14 countries where the Bank used a blend of adjustment and investment operations. Efforts to integrate environmental concerns were generally effective. The Bank's aid coordination efforts seem to have been productive, with some exceptions, but there were shortcomings in promoting stakeholder participation and, most important, in combating corruption.

A recent study by the ECA Region of power sector reforms (World Bank forthcoming) found that in the most aggressive reformers, subsidies to utilities appear to be falling; tariffs have risen, along with revenues per kilowatt-hour, for public and private operators; and reforms slightly improved energy efficiency in power plants. However, electricity expenditures as a share of income increased, especially for the poor, suggesting a need for measures to mitigate this adverse impact, and the study also identified a need for more and better monitoring and data to evaluate these results more fully.

The Scorecard project funded by ESMAP in 1998[47] provides indicators of progress toward certain key objectives in the energy sector. The Scorecard identifies six central steps: corporatization/commercialization of the state-owned utility; passage of an energy law; start-up of a regulatory body; private sector investment in independent power producers; restructuring/unbundling of the core state-owned utility;

and privatization of part of the state-owned utility. Countries receive 1 point for each of the six steps,

Efforts to integrate environmental concerns were generally effective.

so countries that have taken all six steps receive a score of 6.[48] Although results are available for all segments of the energy sector, electric power is used in this evaluation as a proxy for energy sector reform, since that sector is uniformly significant in all the countries. The reform indicators for 24 transition countries confirm the priority given to commercialization, corporatization, and unbundling, which were objectives in 22 of the countries; 16 had taken steps toward commercialization and corporatization, and 13 toward restructuring by mid-1998. Only 10 countries had regulation as an explicit objective, and 11 had taken that step by mid-1998. Three countries had some privatization in the absence of an energy law (Russia) or without a law or a regulator (Bosnia and Herzegovina, Kazakhstan).

Figure 2.5 shows the reform scores for each country, superimposed on a chart showing the change in their energy efficiency between 1992 and 2000. Four countries (Armenia, Georgia, Hungary, and Poland) received a score of 6. They are among the countries showing the greatest improvement in energy efficiency, and they are also among the eight countries where this evaluation judged the outcome of the programmatic approach followed by the Bank to be fair to good.[49] The one country where the outcome was poor (Romania) has a score of zero, but there was substantial reform subsequently. The other countries with a zero score are Azerbaijan, Kyrgyz Republic, Slovak Republic, Tajikistan, and Uzbekistan; their performance in energy efficiency has been mixed. The average number of steps taken by the group of 24 as a whole is 2.83; that is, they had on average taken less than half of the requisite steps toward energy sector reform. Compared with other Regions of the Bank in mid-1998, the 24 countries come out behind the Latin America and the Caribbean Region and the South Asia Region on the reform scorecard, but ahead of the Africa, East Asia and Pacific, and Middle East and North Africa Regions.

The evidence on sequencing of reforms is ambiguous in ECA, as it is in other regions (OED,

OEG, and OEU 2003a). The Region's own review of power sector reform and private participation concluded that the push for unbundling and privatization was premature (as in Ukraine) and, in general, attempts to leap from a totally non-commercial state-owned entity to private commercial utilities did not work (Krishnaswamy and Stuggins 2002). However, in some cases (Kazakhstan and Central European countries) "leapfrogging" to privatization as a means to achieve commercialization did lead to positive sector change, and even where this approach was not fully successful, service quality and coverage have tended to improve.

Of course, the indicators of overall progress do not necessarily measure the relative importance of Bank assistance. OED reviews indicate that the Bank's involvement in Hungary's energy sector probably had beneficial effects on the progress toward restructuring and privatization, although it is likely that the government would have implemented the reforms in any case. Privatization of coal mines in Russia was a highly complex task carried out in an environment of difficult political and industrial relations, and might not have been possible without strong government commitment and efforts to consult important stakeholders, together with Bank flexibility in the design and implementation of projects. Closure of loss-making mines in Russia reduced budgetary subsidies for the coal sector from over 1 percent of GDP in 1993 to under 0.1 percent by 2001, and such economic benefits were also found in Poland and Ukraine (OED, OEG, and OEU 2003b). Inadequate government commitment and consensus appears to have limited progress in privatizing Poland's coal sector, but a review of PSD in energy in Poland found a clear association, if not causality, between the Bank program and most of the institutional changes in the subsectors affected by Bank projects. Bank performance was rated as satisfactory in 89 percent of the projects reviewed for this study, but this statistic, which is

Privatization of coal mines in Russia might not have been possible without strong government commitment and efforts to consult important stakeholders, together with Bank flexibility.

| Figure 2.5 | Change in GDP per Unit of Energy Use, 1992–00, and Energy Reform Score, 1998 |

1995 US$ per kg. oil equivalent

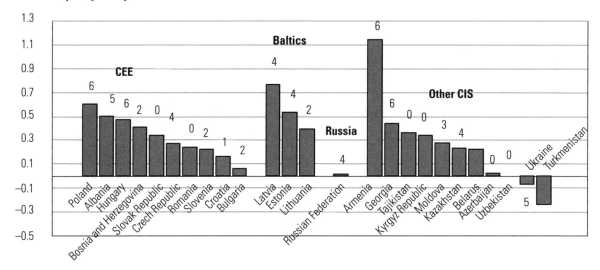

Source: WDI and World Bank, 1999.

significantly higher than the ratings given to Bank performance in all projects Bankwide, does not lend itself to any conclusions about the link between the Bank's role and country outcomes.[50] It does, however, support the Region's view that the Bank succeeded in fundamentally changing the debate in the ECA transition countries from whether or not to carry out certain reforms to when they should be undertaken.

Rehabilitation, emergency relief, and critical imports accounted for over one-third of the 102 energy projects. Given conditions at the start of the transition period, the Bank may well have been right to emphasize these objectives at first. However, difficulties in attaining the objectives in as many as two-thirds of the projects, particularly because of procurement problems and conflicts between short- and long-run objectives, point to *three key lessons for project design. First, intensive efforts to pre-identify critical import needs are usually inadequate to enable a new borrower to administer the Bank's procurement regulations—negative lists are preferable. Second, the Bank should not count on project implementation units to resolve difficulties in implementing standard procurement and disbursement procedures.*[51] Institutional capacity can be strengthened through on-the-job training of local counterparts, and assistance with procurement matters can be best provided through specialists based in Bank resident missions. *Third, rehabilitation-type projects should not be encumbered with long-term reform objectives, either formal or informal.*[52]

Reform of the energy sector was linked with a broader need for reform in other sectors, and also with the profound political, economic, social, and institutional changes taking place at widely different rates in the economies in transition. That linkage had important implications for the Bank's lending and non-lending operations. *Four main lessons emerge for the longer term. First, energy sector reform is not in itself sufficient to deal with some key problems,* such as the elimination of subsidies to energy sector entities; increased discipline in metering, billing, and collecting payments; reforming pricing policy; and closing uneconomic energy production facilities.[53] Reforms such as tariff policy must go hand in hand with control of the macroeconomic situation. In such circumstances, *the Bank appropriately chose to apply a blend of lending instruments in many countries,* including structural adjustment, sector adjustment, specific investment, technical assistance, emergency recovery, and programmatic structural adjustment loans. Moreover, lending was *usually accompanied by ESW.*[54]

Second, energy sector reform is a complex and long-term process that must alter deep-rooted incentive systems and cultural attitudes, as well as institutions and markets. In some countries, accession to the EU is a strong motivating factor to maintain sound economic policies, but it was unrealistic to expect restructuring and privatization to overcome legal, political, attitudinal, and payment obstacles and be immune to destabilizing macroeconomic factors. Regulatory reforms are essential, but are not sufficient. *Improving commercial performance and corporate and sectoral governance are primary, regardless of sector structures and ownership. Whether privatization is feasible as an immediate option to achieve these goals depends on country circumstances. The Bank needs to develop operational guidance as to what sequence of reforms and interventions works best in particular country situations.*[55]

Third, because of the complexity and long-term nature of energy sector reform, borrowers usually require TA to help them design and implement the necessary measures. In one case, OED suggested that Bank coal sector restructuring programs in transition countries should include TA to familiarize local technical experts with modern, cost-saving procedures for closing mines. Transition countries have generally resisted borrowing for TA, but the Bank must continue to stress its importance and seek ways to supply it. Field office staff can play an important role in ensuring the success of a major reform program through effective day-to-day management of operations.

Finally, it is highly desirable to foster the participation of a wide cross-section of society in

Energy sector reform is not in itself sufficient to deal with some key problems.

the reform of the energy sector. Variations on this lesson are reported in more than half the countries with energy lending, and it probably constitutes the most common lesson, also found in other sectors. In its most obvious version, it refers to the importance of borrower commitment to and ownership of the reforms, but it also extends to seeking, identifying, and working with "champions" in strategic decisionmaking positions, explaining the purpose of the reforms to the most affected parties and trying to soften the impact on the most vulnerable social groups.

These lessons suggest an approach to lending that might be applied to countries with poor or damaged infrastructure and energy sectors still dominated by state-owned enterprises. Initially, quick-disbursing rehabilitation and emergency recovery operations would tackle the shortage of critical supplies and the need for urgent restoration and maintenance of facilities. Disbursement formalities would be kept to a minimum—for ex-

ample, working from a "negative" list rather than trying to pre-identify critical imports. Little or no policy conditionality would be involved, although ESW and the policy dialogue would be conducted intensively from the beginning, along with training and TA (both in addition to and as part of the ESW). Furthermore, significant efforts would be devoted at this early stage to donor coordination and building stakeholder participation. The latter would help frame the TA and lending, which would move from emergency operations to a combination of investment and adjustment projects. The timing of critical policy measures should benefit considerably from stakeholder involvement, especially that of key counterparts, who could help evaluate alternatives and choose the timing of politically difficult decisions. Projects would deal with corruption and ensure that the foundations of good governance are laid in the sector entities as a preparation for later privatization.

Lessons and Recommendations

The Bank shared the optimism of many early reformers and Western observers about the speed with which economic liberalization and legal and policy changes would produce robust supply responses in the transition economies—particularly those of the CIS—and consequently about the depth and duration of the initial declines in output and employment and the related social costs and political turbulence. In large part, this optimism was related to the expectation that the rapid shift of control over resources to private hands, along with the liberalization of prices and trade, would lead quickly to more rational resource use under market discipline.

But this did not happen in many countries. Meanwhile, the Bank, along with other donors, greatly underestimated the impact of corruption and of the weakness of core institutions and public administrations in managing the transition process, and did not address these areas adequately in its assistance programs. *An appropriate institutional and regulatory framework and a capable, transparent public sector are central elements of an efficient, market-oriented private sector. Analytical work on governance and public sector management should precede large amounts of Bank lending, particularly in situations where obvious problems are likely to affect assistance programs.*

Poverty has also been a far more serious problem than the Bank expected in countries making the transition from plan to market, most notably in the CIS. *In the future the Bank can be much better prepared to identify and address rapidly growing poverty by monitoring poverty levels as a priority from the very beginning of its involvement in a country.*

The transition from a centrally planned economy requires a vast web of interrelated changes in attitudes and concepts as well as laws, policies, and institutions. One of the key generic lessons that emerges from evaluations of the transition experience is that *a carefully crafted external assistance program can help to design and implement these changes and ameliorate their social costs, but however well designed a program of reform, the rate of progress will be largely*

The transition from a centrally planned economy requires a vast web of interrelated changes in attitudes and concepts as well as laws, policies, and institutions.

determined by the government's ownership of it and the degree of consensus it is able to mobilize in the society at large. A well-informed civil society can also be a major "driver" for change, and stakeholder analysis is an important input to understanding the political and social processes at work in a country that can have a major impact on the outcome of assistance. The growing Bank emphasis on stakeholder participation—for example, in the preparation of CASs and PRSPs—is a move in the right direction; many other specific examples can be found, as this approach becomes mainstreamed in all forms of Bank assistance (box 3.1).

A related theme that emerges from OED assessments of Bank assistance to the transition economies has been the limited capacity of most of the borrowing governments to design and implement complex and difficult programs and legal structures and the tendency of the Bank to underestimate the duration and intensity of the assistance needed. *Rehabilitation and other projects with short-term objectives should be de-*

APLS and LILs, along with the effective use of TA, can be used to promote policy reform and institutional change over the longer term.

signed to minimize delays (use negative lists rather than trying to pre-identify critical imports); do without project implementation units; and forego long-term reform objectives. Beyond the short term, capacity building should be central to any country strategy. [1]

OED's *2001 Annual Review of Development Effectiveness* (OED 2002a) found that stand-alone TA loans fared better than any other form of lending in countries with low ratings for policy and institutional environment, particularly in the ECA Region, suggesting that the Bank should focus on creating capacity and institution building in these countries. However, many (particularly CIS) countries are averse to borrowing for TA, often leaving it to bilateral grants, which have been less successful. The Bank provides TA through other means as well, such as collaborative project preparation and ESW, and borrowers value this contribution.

A number of relatively new Bank instruments, such as APLS and LILs, along with the effective use of TA, can be used to promote policy reform and institutional change over the longer term. Experience has demonstrated the lengthy time often needed for ownership and consensus to emerge and the importance of learning from

---

Box 3.1   Stakeholder Participation

A key element of the Bank's country strategy implementation in the Ukraine was a significant market reform education and awareness program. The Resident Mission, along with the World Bank Institute, carried out a program of seminars, workshops, and roundtable discussions with government officials, parliamentarians, academics, and others on the need for reform, the nature and objectives of the reform, and the benefits and outcomes likely to result. The director for Ukraine, Belarus, and Moldova has instituted stakeholder analysis for all projects. Public information campaigns in Armenia for judicial reform and in Bulgaria for pension reform facilitated implementation by ensuring that policies were widely acceptable to the people. Preparation of the 2002 Albania CAS included consultation with representatives of civil society and the private sector, as well as with par-

liamentarians. In Lithuania the Structural Adjustment Loan team briefed multi-party committees throughout the period of parliamentary elections. Intensive dialogue between the government, mining companies, and trade unions, and the participation of the unions in program design, contributed significantly to the successful implementation of the employment restructuring program in the Poland Coal Sectoral Adjustment Loan. Both OED and QAG have praised the Bank's work in Russia's coal sector, in particular its extensive consultations with stakeholders. In the Bank's Structural Adjustment Participatory Review Initiative (SAPRI), Hungary was one of seven countries in which civil organizations were included with the Bank and governments to assess and analyze the economic and social impacts of adjustment lending (Báger [2002] describes this exercise and its results).

experience. *Perhaps the most important component of a successful strategy for supporting transition is flexibility. Political and social analysis should play a role, along with economic and institutional analysis, to identify problems and develop solutions along the way.*

ESW plays an important role, not only in ensuring that lending operations are based on sound country knowledge, but also in informing public debate on the issues of transition. It is valued by borrowers, sometimes above financial assistance. *Given its importance to the Bank's country dialogues and to the design of country strategies and projects, all ESW, including informal reports, should be subjected to more systematic retrospective evaluation of both quality and impact, and an effective strategy for its dissemination should be an integral part of the Bank's country assistance strategies.*[2] *Borrower participation in carrying out ESW can be an effective means of building capacity in a country.*[3]

Aid coordination in ECA still falls well short of the ideal, at the level of both policy and implementation (box 3.2). The conflicts, duplication, and lack of an agreed development agenda in some countries reduce the effectiveness of all donors. The goal should be to *help governments define clear development strategies, with mon-* *itorable action plans to implement them; these would provide the framework for the donors to agree with the*

Aid coordination in ECA still falls well short of the ideal.

government on how much external support is *to be provided, by whom, and for what,* with a view to avoiding overlaps and allowing donors to specialize in sectors or areas where they have both a special interest and the relevant expertise. *Ideally the process is led and coordinated by the recipient government.*[4] The PRSP is improving the alignment between donors and recipient countries for the poorest countries, but OED's joint evaluation of the Comprehensive Development Framework found that the transaction costs of delivering aid remain high and donors continue to engage in unproductive competition (CDF Secretariat 2003). The donors need to identify one among them to be the main partner for a particular sector, program, or project, to lead the policy dialogue in that area and assist the government in coordinating the donor contributions, both technical and financial.

Chapter 2 of this report identified a number of sectoral and thematic areas where the Bank needs to *define clearer strategies* for assistance, *differentiated by the state of governance and institutional capacity* in each country:

Box 3.2   Aid Coordination

As laid out by the Bank and the Development Assistance Committee (DAC) of the Organization for Economic Cooperation and Development, aid coordination should integrate external assistance with the development priorities of the recipient; responsibility for coordination should reside primarily with the recipient government; and both recipients and donors should adhere to strategic objectives and investment programs (OED 2001). CAEs present a mixed picture of the quality of aid coordination in the transition countries, but provide no examples of countries meeting the DAC criteria. Few if any of the transition country governments are equipped to provide the necessary framework for coordination, and often they do not view this as a priority; their interest lies mainly in resource mobilization.

The absence of an integrated development agenda paves the way for supply-driven assistance, with each donor focusing on areas it feels are most important, often with little consultation with the government or with other donors, and, in some cases, competing with other donors or financing activities with conflicting objectives. Such instances are common, for example, in financial intermediary loans, where other agencies have funded credit lines with lower interest rates than those required in Bank loans, or sponsored narrowly directed credit lines in conflict with Bank efforts to convince governments to phase out the use of directed credit. Provision of technical assistance by bilateral grants, in conjunction with Bank projects, has often proven not to be useful, particularly when it is tied to national suppliers.

- *Legal and judicial reform* is critical for improvements in the business climate (company law, collateral laws, security laws, bankruptcy laws, anti-monopoly laws, respect for private property, contractual rights), the financial sector (banking and central banking, bankruptcy, collateral, failed bank resolution), social protection (labor laws), and governance in general. The focus should be on implementation as much as on the passage of laws.
- Improved governance, including *transparency*, can increase public accountability and discourage corruption. The Bank should go out of its way to make its own studies and documents public and should encourage governments to report more regularly and more fully to their parliaments and to the public at large. The use of information and communications technology has tremendous potential to increase public accountability.
- Given the alternative models for *pension reform*, a clear strategic approach is needed, differentiated by the ability of the country to administer and fund the system.
- Improved commercial performance and corporate and sectoral governance should be the primary objectives for *enterprises in the energy sector.* The sequencing of reforms, including the feasibility of immediate privatization, depends on country circumstances. Some operational guidance is needed on what sequence of reforms and interventions works best in particular country situations.

Chapter 2 also identified a number of other areas that warrant greater attention:

- Additional efforts are needed to *assess and improve the business climate*, particularly by removing barriers to the entry of new firms and creating incentives for firms to move out of the informal sector; providing a capable, transparent public sector; and strengthening the financial sector.
- The emphasis in *future privatizations* should, when circumstances permit, be on more measured, better prepared transactions and on helping governments follow a transparent, competitive process open to foreign participation. For firms that continue to drain public resources and whose sale and restructuring

have proven to be difficult, greater attention is needed to the design of rule-based administrative procedures to initiate their liquidation.
- Additional measures to *strengthen the financial sector* include enforcement of prudential regulations, including limits on loan concentration and related-party lending; training for bank supervisors, lawyers and judges, accountants and auditors, and other skilled professionals; and for state-owned banks, stronger governance, tighter budget constraints, divestiture of branches, and restrictions on the scope of banking licenses. Progress in increasing the effectiveness of bank supervision and in not just adopting, but also enforcing, international accounting standards should be among the triggers for financial sector lending.
- Financial sector staff should be involved in the *design of all financial intermediary loans* and should ensure that the factors important to sustainability are adequately taken into account. Microfinance projects should give greater attention to developing savings services and should incorporate a donor exit strategy from the start.
- *Reform of social assistance programs* (other than pensions) should include capacity building to help national institutions analyze needs, develop a policy consensus, and improve targeting of benefits; administrative reforms to improve collections, targeting and efficiency; and actions in areas that have proven to be barriers to social protection reform in virtually every transition economy—labor laws that encourage labor hoarding among declining firms and discourage hiring among expanding firms, strategies for sharing fiscal and policy burdens of assistance programs among different levels of government, and problems in coverage and administration caused by the growth of informal sectors.
- *Energy sector reform* is not in itself sufficient to deal with all the problems affecting the sector, such as the elimination of subsidies to energy sector entities; increasing discipline in metering, billing, and collecting payments; reforming pricing policies; and closing uneconomic energy production facilities. A blend of instruments, including investment, adjustment, technical assistance, and programmatic lending, as well as ESW, can support the necessary elements of reform.

ANNEX A: SUPPLEMENTARY TABLES

Table A.1	Number of IBRD/IDA Approved Projects for Transition Countries, FY89–03

	1989	1990	1991	1992	1993	1994	1995	1996	1997	1998	1999	2000	2001	2002	2003
CEE	3	8	13	10	15	19	17	21	26	33	29	23	26	18	17
Baltic States					3	4	8	5	7	1	5	4	3	3	1
Russia					4	6	9	9	8	3	3	2	5	2	5
Other CIS					4	12	22	24	24	28	34	14	18	17	19
Total	3	8	13	10	26	41	56	59	65	65	71	43	52	40	42

Source: World Bank data.

Table A.2	IBRD/IDA Commitments to Transition Countries, by Instrument, FY 89–03

	Adjustment		Investment		Total	
Country	# Projects	$ million	# Projects	$ million	# Projects	$ million
Central and Eastern Europe						
Albania	7	170	42	530	49	700
Bosnia-Herzegovina	6	339	36	495	42	834
Bulgaria	11	1,051	19	751	30	1,801
Croatia	2	297	18	740	20	1,037
Czech Republic	1	450	2	326	3	776
Hungary	5	1,025	19	1,677	24	2,702
Macedonia, FYR	6	319	19	311	25	631
Poland	7	1,820	30	3,565	37	5,385
Romania	6	1,680	32	2,120	38	3,800
Slovak Republic	2	257	3	84	5	341
Slovenia	1	80	4	98	5	178
Total	54	7,488	224	10,696	278	18,184
Baltic States						
Estonia	1	30	7	121	8	151
Latvia	4	166	15	250	19	416
Lithuania	3	239	14	252	17	491
Total	8	434	36	623	44	1,058
Russia						
Russian Federation						
Total	9	6,320	47	6,821	56	13,141
Other CIS						
Armenia	6	335	23	401	29	736
Azerbaijan	3	202	17	395	20	597
Belarus	1	120	3	73	4	193
Georgia	5	280	27	445	32	725
Kazakhstan	5	1,070	18	854	23	1,924
Kyrgyz Republic	8	346	19	304	27	649
Moldova	5	295	16	234	21	529
Tajikistan	4	167	14	155	18	322
Turkmenistan			3	90	3	90
Ukraine	7	2,260	19	1,263	26	3,523
Uzbekistan	1	160	12	439	13	599
Total	45	5,234	171	4,653	216	9,887
Overall result	116	19,477	478	22,793	594	42,269

Source: World Bank data.

Table A.3		IBRD/IDA Commitments to Transition Countries, by Sector, FY89–03	
By number of projects		**By $ million**	
Sector	**# Projects**	**Sector**	**$ million**
1 Rural	84	1 Economic policy	10,638
2 Energy and mining	66	2 Energy and mining	7,061
3 Economic policy	66	3 Transport	4,077
4 Transport	56	4 Rural	3,957
5 Public sector governance	55	5 Financial	3,571
6 Social protection	52	6 Public sector governance	2,597
7 Financial sector	37	7 Private sector development	2,431
8 Health, nutrition and population	35	8 Social protection	2,305
9 Private sector development	35	9 Health, nutrition and population	1,468
10 Education	27	10 Urban development	1,327
11 Urban development	25	11 Education	1,162
12 Water supply and sanitation	23	12 Water supply and sanitation	759
13 Environment	20	13 Global information/communications technology	483
14 Global information/communications technology	7	14 Environment	393
15 Social development	6	15 Social development	42
Total	**594**	**Total**	**42,269**

Source: World Bank data.

Table A.4 Total Receipts by Source, Official and Private, 1989–01 (US$ million)

	1989	1990	1991	1992	1993	1994	1995	1996	1997	1998	1999	2000	2001	Total
Central Europe and Baltics														
EC+EU members	7	7,579	5,617	8,016	4,812	5,443	11,909	9,731	11,663	24,085	25,503	23,823	18,074	156,262
Other bilateral	0	1,537	255	1,103	3,218	1,334	3,065	2,271	3,148	1,608	244	−160	686	18,309
IBRD+IDA+IFC	0	186	825	1,018	968	1,339	606	543	913	243	905	860	416	8,822
EBRD	0	0	0	163	312	614	1,040	893	511	624	313	114	688	5,272
AS. D B	0	0	0	0	0	0	0	0	0	0	0	0	0	0
SAF & ESAF	0	0	0	0	12	22	11	0	25	20	18	14	4	126
Other multilaterals	3	39	23	26	26	190	49	83	54	73	85	118	77	845
Total	**10**	**9,340**	**6,719**	**10,326**	**9,348**	**8,944**	**16,679**	**13,520**	**16,314**	**26,653**	**27,068**	**24,770**	**19,946**	**189,636**
Russia														
EC+EU members	0	254	822	5,412	8,406	4,318	3,214	3,508	4,128	7,360	1,348	727	3,773	43,270
Other bilateral	0	0	561	1,745	1,729	44	852	122	922	721	2,350	1,779	512	11,337
IBRD+IDA+IFC	0	0	0	1	431	285	836	1,096	2,682	1,171	425	297	26	7,249
EBRD				4	123	77	214	456	435	501	−45	−172	190	1,782
AS. D B														
SAF & ESAF														
Other multilaterals	0	0	0	1	3	11	22	12	11	11	19	21	37	147
Total	**0**	**254**	**1,383**	**7,163**	**10,692**	**4,735**	**5,138**	**5,194**	**8,177**	**9,764**	**4,096**	**2,652**	**4,538**	**63,785**
Other CIS														
EC+EU members	0	289	9,101	9,420	2,881	1,831	728	663	717	−363	70	25	160	25,521
Other bilaterals	0	0	1,933	329	773	829	645	1,540	1,627	3,938	1,467	2,463	2,807	18,352
IBRD+IDA+IFC	0	0	0	−1	−31	459	996	872	786	837	975	250	577	5,720
EBRD	0	0	0	−2	−18	67	110	145	158	206	176	161	262	1,265
AS. D B	0	0	0	0	0	3	110	59	124	173	118	115	102	803
SAF & ESAF	0	0	0	0	0	14	46	153	221	178	126	70	89	896
Other multilaterals	0	0	1	4	35	71	87	52	48	55	72	81	87	593
Total	**0**	**289**	**11,036**	**9,750**	**3,640**	**3,274**	**2,722**	**3,484**	**3,681**	**5,024**	**3,005**	**3,163**	**4,085**	**53,150**

Source: OECD/DAC CD-ROM: Geographical Distribution of Financial Flows to Aid Recipients (1960–01).

Table A.5 GDP Per Capita of Transition Countries (constant 1995 US$), FY89–02

Country name	1989	1990	1991	1992	1993	1994	1995	1996	1997	1998	1999	2000	2001	2002
Central and Eastern Europe														
Albania	942	842	607	**563**	621	687	761	841	789	853	914	979	1,032	1,071
Bosnia and Herzegovina	..	..	..	..	..	**425**	546	981	1,298	1,455	1,551	1,595	1,632	1,671
Bulgaria	1,855	1,716	1,587	1,487	1,477	1,511	1,560	1,421	**1,349**	1,412	1,453	1,547	1,652	1,733
Croatia	..	5,438	4,282	3,783	**3,481**	3,686	4,059	4,402	4,785	4,961	4,943	5,078	5,269	5,549
Czech Republic	..	5,270	4,682	**4,588**	4,608	4,731	5,037	5,288	5,226	5,177	5,207	5,381	5,574	5,691
Hungary	5,018	4,858	4,288	4,165	**4,153**	4,289	4,367	4,441	4,662	4,908	5,136	5,372	5,540	5,735
Macedonia, FYR	..	2,741	2,765	2,571	2,369	2,311	**2,263**	2,270	2,286	2,351	2,441	2,541	2,415	2,418
Poland	..	2,604	**2,414**	2,469	2,557	2,684	2,888	3,038	3,242	3,396	3,536	3,678	3,716	3,762
Romania	1,808	1,702	1,484	**1,377**	1,399	1,457	1,564	1,632	1,536	1,466	1,451	1,462	1,541	1,611
Slovak Republic	4,322	4,217	3,603	3,346	**3,211**	3,363	3,570	3,771	3,977	4,129	4,180	4,267	4,405	4,595
Slovenia	..	9,659	8,784	**8,331**	8,694	9,053	9,419	9,744	10,218	10,624	11,160	11,653	11,978	12,326
Baltic States														
Estonia	4,861	4,514	4,175	3,351	**3,151**	3,154	3,348	3,531	3,921	4,143	4,148	4,464	4,708	5,000
Latvia	3,731	3,703	3,328	2,193	**1,900**	1,941	1,950	2,035	2,242	2,388	2,476	2,666	2,893	3,100
Lithuania	..	3,005	2,830	2,231	1,878	**1,706**	1,824	1,925	2,074	2,241	2,215	2,320	2,488	2,659
Russia														
Russian Federation	3,794	3,666	3,473	2,967	2,713	2,375	2,280	2,208	2,235	**2,131**	2,255	2,471	2,609	2,734
Other CIS														
Armenia	..	1,542	1,367	804	**745**	799	868	934	979	1,066	1,114	1,193	1,317	1,495
Azerbaijan	..	..	..	601	455	361	315	**315**	331	360	383	422	460	505
Belarus	..	1,583	1,563	1,410	1,300	1,149	**1,033**	1,066	1,192	1,298	1,347	1,429	1,502	1,579
Georgia	1,449	1,232	973	538	382	**344**	355	396	439	453	468	479	505	537
Kazakhstan	2,094	1,985	1,756	1,656	1,507	1,332	**1,240**	1,258	1,293	1,287	1,342	1,497	1,717	1,893
Kyrgyz Republic	642	665	603	514	435	348	**325**	343	372	374	382	399	417	411
Moldova	1,817	1,769	1,486	1,056	1,044	721	713	673	686	643	**623**	638	678	729
Tajikistan	1,215	1,179	1,063	740	611	472	407	**334**	335	346	357	384	420	453
Turkmenistan	2,614	2,569	2,330	2,088	1,807	1,438	1,296	1,179	**1,017**	1,057	1,194	1,354	1,587	1,787
Ukraine	2,108	1,969	1,800	1,621	1,390	1,076	953	864	845	**835**	840	896	986	1,038
Uzbekistan	614	611	596	517	493	459	446	**445**	460	472	485	497	511	525

Note: In bold: The year of the lowest GDP per capita.
Source: WDI database as of August 2003.

Table A.6	Social Indicators								
Country	**Poverty headcount index ($2.15/day), latest year 1995–99**	**Gini coefficient for income per capita**		**Life expectancy at birth, total (years)**		**Mortality rate, infant (per 1,000 live births)**		**Basic education gross enroll-ment rate (% of 6/7–14/15 age group)**	
		1987–90	1996–99	1990	2001	1990	2001	1989–90	1996–97
Albania	11.5	..	0.27	72	74	37	23	90.8	87.6
Armenia	43.5	0.27	0.59	72	74	50	31	95.5	82.9
Azerbaijan	23.5	..	..	71	65	84	77	89.5	96.6
Belarus	1	0.23	0.28	71	68	18	17	95.8	94.1
Bosnia and Herzegovina	..	..	..	71	74	18	15	..	..
Bulgaria	3.1	0.23	0.41	71	72	15	14	98.4	94.0
Croatia	0.2	0.36	0.35	72	74	11	7	96.0	89.0
Czech Republic	0	0.19	0.25	72	75	11	4	97.6	99.1
Estonia	2.1	0.24	0.37	69	71	12	11	96.2	93.7
FYR Macedonia	6.7	..	0.37	72	73	32	22	89.4	86.9
Georgia	18.9	0.29	0.43	72	73	24	24	95.2	80.7
Hungary	1.3	0.21	0.25	69	72	15	8	99.0	99.2
Kazakhstan	5.7	0.3	0.35	68	63	42	81	93.9	89.2
Kyrgyz Republic	49.1	0.31	0.47	68	66	68	52	92.5	89.2
Latvia	6.6	0.24	0.32	69	70	14	17	95.8	90.7
Lithuania	3.1	0.23	0.34	71	73	10	8	94.0	95.8
Moldova	55.4	0.27	0.42	68	67	30	27	95.8	91.6
Poland	1.2	0.28	0.33	71	74	19	8	97.9	98.0
Romania	6.8	0.23	0.3	70	70	27	19	93.6	95.0
Russian Federation	18.8	0.26	0.47	69	66	17	18	93.0	90.8
Slovak Republic	2.6	..	..	71	73	12	8	96.8	96.3
Slovenia	0	0.22	0.25	73	76	8	4	96.1	99.8
Tajikistan	68.3	0.28	0.47	69	67	98	91	94.1	85.5
Turkmenistan	7	0.28	0.45	66	65	80	69	94.3	83.1
Ukraine	3	0.24	0.33	70	68	18	17	92.8	90.7
Uzbekistan	..	..	..	69	67	53	52	92.2	89.7

Sources: Poverty headcount and Gini coefficient from World Bank 2000c. Life expectancy and mortality rate from WDI. Enrollment rates from World Bank 2003.

Table A.7 Progress in Transition by Country, 1994–03

Country	Population (millions) 2001	Private sector share of GDP (EBRD estimate, %) 1994	Private 2002	Large-scale privatization 1994	Large-scale 2003	Small-scale privatization 1994	Small-scale 2003	Governance and enterprise restructuring 1994	Governance 2003	Price liberalization 1994	Price 2003	Trade and foreign exchange system 1994	Trade 2003	Competition policy 1994	Competition 2003	Banking reform and interest rate liberalization 1994	Banking 2003	Securities markets and non-bank financial institutions 1994	Securities 2003	Infrastructure reform 1994	Infrastructure 2003
Albania	3.4	50	75	1	2+	3	4	2	2	4-	4-	4	4+	1	2-	2	2+	1	2-	1	2
Armenia	3.0	40	70	1	3+	2+	4-	1	2+	4-	4+	2	4+	1	2	1	2+	1	2	1+	2+
Azerbaijan	8.1	20	60	1	2	1	4-	1	2+	4-	4-	1	4-	1	2	1	2+	1	2-	1	2-
Belarus	10.0	15	20	2-	1	2	2+	1	1	3-	3-	1	2+	2	2	1	2-	2	2	1	1+
Bosnia and Herzegovina	4.3		45	1	2+	2	3	1	2	1	4	1	4-	1	1	1	2+	1	2-	1	2+
Bulgaria	8.1	40	70	2	4-	2	4-	2	3-	4	4+	4	4+	2	2+	2	3+	1	2+	1+	3-
Croatia	4.6	40	60	2	3+	4	4+	2	3-	4	4	4	4+	1	2+	3-	4-	2	3-	2-	3-
Czech Republic	10.3	65	80	4	4	4	4+	3	3+	4	4	4	4+	3-	3	3	4-	3-	3	2+	3
Estonia	1.4	55	80	3	4	4	4+	3	3+	4	4	4	4+	2	3-	3	4-	2-	3+	2	3+
FR Yugoslavia	8.6		40	1	2+	3	3	1	2	2-	4	1	3+	1	1	1	2+	1	2	1+	2
FYR Macedonia	2.0	35	60	2	3	4	4	2	2+	4	4+	4	4+	1	2	2	3	1	2-	1+	2
Georgia	5.4	20	65	1	3+	2	4	1	2	4-	4+	1	4+	1	2	1	2+	1	2-	1	2+
Hungary	10.0	55	80	3	4	4-	4+	3	3+	4+	4+	4+	4+	3	3	3	4	2	4-	3-	4-
Kazakhstan	14.9	20	65	2	3	2+	4	1	2	3-	4	2	3+	1	2+	1	3	2-	2+	1	2+
Kyrgyz Republic	4.7	30	60	3	3	4	4	2	2	4+	4+	3	4+	2	2	1	2+	1	2	1+	1+
Latvia	2.4	55	70	2	3+	4	4+	2	3	4+	4+	4	4+	2	3-	3	4-	2	3	2	3-
Lithuania	3.7	50	75	3	4-	4	4+	2	3	4	4	4	4+	2	3	2	3	2	3	1	3-
Moldova	4.3	20	50	2	3	2	3+	2	2-	4-	4-	2	4-	2-	2	2	2+	2	2	1	2
Poland	38.7	55	75	3	3+	4	4+	3	3+	4	4+	4	4+	3	3	3	3+	2	4-	2	3+
Romania	22.3	35	65	2	3+	2+	4-	2	2	4-	4+	4	4	1	2+	2	3-	2	2	2	3
Russian Federation	145.4	50	70	3	3+	3	4	2-	2+	4-	3+	3	4+	2	2+	2	2	2	3-	2-	2+
Slovak Republic	5.4	55	80	3	4	4	4+	3	3	4	4	4	4+	3	3	3-	3+	3-	3-	1	2+
Slovenia	2.0	30	65	2	3	4	4+	3-	3	4-	4	4	4+	2	3-	3	3+	3-	3-	2-	3
Tajikistan	6.2	15	50	1	2+	2	4-	1	2-	2+	3-	1	3+	2	2-	1	2-	1	1	1	1+
Turkmenistan	5.4	15	25	1	1	2	2	1	1	2+	3-	1	1	2	1	1	1	1	1	1	1
Ukraine	49.3	30	65	1	3	2	4	1	2	3-	4	1	3	2	2+	1	2+	2-	2	1	2
Uzbekistan	25.0	20	45	2	3-	3	3	1	2-	4-	3-	2	2-	2	2	1	2-	2	2	1	2-

Source: EBRD data.

51

Table A.8	CAE Ratings for Transition Countries through FY03			
Country	Dates	Outcome	Institutional development impact	Sustainability
Albania	1992–97	MU	M	U
Azerbaijan	1995–98	MU	M	L
Bulgaria	1991–97	U	NR	NR
	1998–01	S	M	L
Kazakhstan	1990–99	MS	M	U
Kyrgyz Republic	1993–00	MS	S	U
Lithuania	1991–02	S	H	HL
Poland	1989–96	S	S	L
Russia	1992–98	U	NR	NR
	1999–01	S	M	L
Ukraine	1992–98	MU	M	U

Note: Outcome: S = satisfactory, MS = moderately satisfactory, MU = moderately unsatisfactory, U = unsatisfactory.

Institutional development impact: H = high, S = substantial, M = modest.

Sustainability: HL = highly likely, L = likely, U = uncertain.

NR = not rated.

Source: OED.

Table A.9	OED Project Ratings by Country, Approved FY89–03							

Country	Total [a] evaluated (no.)	Outcome (% sat.)	Sustaina-bility (% likely)	Inst. dev. impact (% subst.)	Total [a] evaluated ($m)	Outcome (% sat.)	Sustaina-bility (% likely)	Inst. dev. impact (% subst.)
Central and Eastern Europe								
Albania	25	84	68	48	337.8	88	67	45
Bosnia-Herzegovina	26	100	83	42	506.0	100	80	56
Bulgaria	20	80	78	53	1,049.0	95	83	43
Croatia	10	90	90	50	482.0	83	98	45
Czech Republic	6	100	83	67	661.7	100	100	98
Hungary	24	88	91	58	2,003.0	96	94	71
Macedonia, FYR	14	79	83	54	403.1	95	73	49
Poland	28	79	74	57	3,214.4	87	90	69
Romania	15	80	87	53	2,003.7	71	76	32
Slovak Republic	3	100	67	100	130.4	100	100	100
Slovenia	5	100	100	75	130.9	100	100	100
Total/ average	**176**	**86**	**81**	**54**	**10,921.9**	**89**	**87**	**60**
Baltic States								
Estonia	7	100	100	86	109.6	100	100	74
Latvia	11	82	90	82	296.5	95	97	77
Lithuania	11	100	90	80	267.5	100	90	74
Total/ average	**29**	**93**	**93**	**82**	**673.5**	**98**	**95**	**75**
Russia								
Russian Federation	26	52	90	36	7,124.9	40	89	23
Total/ average	**26**	**52**	**90**	**36**	**7,124.9**	**40**	**89**	**23**
Other CIS								
Armenia	15	87	86	67	466.5	84	90	75
Azerbaijan	3	67	50	0	148.5	48	44	0
Belarus	5	60	40	60	158.0	5	21	5
Georgia	15	80	93	60	417.1	57	84	47
Kazakhstan	16	81	69	69	1,157.6	97	94	96
Kyrgyz Republic	12	83	58	42	363.3	95	48	39
Moldova	10	70	50	20	316.4	78	46	18
Tajikistan	7	71	57	29	145.3	63	82	42
Turkmenistan	1	0	0	0	21.1	0	0	0
Ukraine	16	87	60	47	2,434.0	96	63	46
Uzbekistan	4	67	33	0	245.6	35	9	0
Total/ average	**104**	**78**	**66**	**48**	**5,873.4**	**84**	**67**	**52**
ECA transition countries [b]	**335**	**82**	**78**	**53**	**24,594**	**74**	**83**	**48**
World Bank overall	2,125	74	62	43	178,811	78	70	46
Low-income								
ECA	**51**	**76**	**65**	**36**	**1,636**	**66**	**53**	**28**
World Bank overall	1,022	66	49	35	69,564	74	61	36
Middle-income								
ECA	**279**	**83**	**80**	**56**	**22,827**	**74**	**85**	**49**
World Bank overall	1,076	81	73	51	108,703	81	76	53

a. The total commitments or number of projects evaluated is not equal to the commitments or projects rated, since some evaluated projects are not rated in all categories. Therefore this column is not necessarily the denominator for the subsequent columns.

b. ECA countries excluding Cyprus, Kosovo, Portugal, Serbia & Montenegro, Turkey, and Yugoslavia.

Source: World Bank data as of February 2004.

| Table A.10 | At-Risk Ratings for Transition Countries, February 2004 |

Country	Number of projects	Net commitment, millions US$	Projects at risk	Projects at risk, %	Commitment at risk, millions US$	Commitment at risk, %
World Bank total	1,323	89,852	252	19	15,596	17
ECA transition countries	243	9,276	43	18	1,692	18
Central and Eastern Europe						
Albania	20	268	2	10	23	9
Bosnia-Herzegovina	19	296	0	0	0	0
Bulgaria	8	241	1	13	14	6
Croatia	11	448	1	9	5	1
Hungary	1	32	0	0	0	0
Macedonia, FYR	8	106	1	13	13	12
Poland	9	994	1	11	38	4
Romania	19	1,145	4	21	175	15
Slovak Republic	5	282	0	0	0	0
Slovenia	2	25	0	0	0	0
Total/ average	102	3,836	10	10	268	7
Baltic States						
Latvia	6	78	0	0	0	0
Lithuania	5	106	1	20	20	19
Total/ average	11	184	1	9	20	11
Russia						
Russian Federation	24	2,043	9	38	779	38
Total/ average	24	2,043	9	38	779	38
Other CIS						
Armenia	13	230	2	15	26	11
Azerbaijan	13	321	1	8	30	9
Belarus	1	23	0	0	0	0
Georgia	16	297	5	31	111	37
Kazakhstan	7	546	0	0	0	0
Kyrgyz Republic	15	272	3	20	70	26
Moldova	12	150	1	8	11	7
Tajikistan	10	166	4	40	95	57
Turkmenistan	0	0	0		0	
Ukraine	11	889	2	18	80	9
Uzbekistan	8	317	5	63	202	64
Total/ average	106	3,213	23	22	626	19

Source: World Bank data.

Table A.11	OED Project Ratings in Transition Countries by Sector, Approved FY89–03						
Sector Board	Total evaluated (# projects)	Outcome (% satisfactory)	Sustaina-bility (% likely)	Institu-tional develop-ment impact (% substantial)	Total evaluated (US$ million)	Outcome (% satisfactory)	Sustaina-bility (% likely)	Institu-tional develop-ment impact (% substantial)
Education	11	82	100	55	347	98	100	91
Energy and mining	41	80	89	50	4,419	74	81	57
Environment	20	95	80	80	78	100	93	100
Economic policy	57	74	77	39	8,556	62	84	29
Financial sector	25	83	79	54	1,787	94	91	81
Global information/ communications technology	6	100	100	67	287	100	100	90
Health, nutrition and population	14	86	86	50	657	93	93	32
Public sector governance	26	92	85	73	1,372	97	82	76
Private sector development	20	80	68	58	1,506	92	91	85
Rural sector	43	72	62	49	2,050	75	55	36
Social protection	26	85	82	62	1,488	44	96	36
Transport	26	88	79	60	1,593	76	87	45
Urban development	12	82	56	18	314	89	71	8
Water supply and sanitation	8	86	60	29	139	92	87	36
Overall result, ECA transition countries	**335**	**82**	**78**	**53**	**24,594**	**74**	**83**	**48**
World Bank overall	**2,125**	**74**	**62**	**43**	**178,811**	**78**	**70**	**46**

Source: World Bank data as of February 2004.

Table A.12	Comparison of Bankwide and ECA Ratings by Sector (percent of net commitments), Approved FY89–03					
Sector Board	Outcome, % sat (Bank)	Outcome, % sat (ECA)	Sustaina-bility, % likely (Bank)	Sustaina-bility, % likely (ECA)	ID impact, % substan-tial (Bank)	ID impact, % substan-tial (ECA)
Education	84	98	74	100	43	91
Energy and mining	71	74	64	81	45	57
Environment	62	100	69	93	39	100
Economic policy	68	62	64	84	34	29
Financial sector	81	94	77	91	55	81
Global information/communications technology	95	100	97	100	64	90
Health, nutrition and population	80	93	78	93	50	32
Public sector governance	86	97	84	82	55	76
Private sector development	88	92	81	91	57	85
Rural sector	79	75	63	55	49	36
Social development	100	a	100	a	100	a
Social protection	88	44	76	96	45	36
Transport	90	76	77	87	63	45
Urban development	83	89	71	71	28	8
Water supply and sanitation	59	92	37	87	25	36
Overall result	**78**	**74**	**70**	**83**	**46**	**48**

a. No projects in ECA.

Source: World Bank data as of February 2004.

Table A.13	Quality of Economic and Sector Work				
	Satisfactory or better (percent)[a]				
	FY98	**FY99**	**FY00**	**FY01**	**FY02**
Bankwide	72	73	86	90	92
AFR	56	47	85	85	94
EAP	75	82	91	96	88
ECA[b]	82	69	90	100	100
LCR	72	89	82	81	77
MNA	100	94	100	89	100
SAR	90	100	78	83	100
	Tasks (number)				
Bankwide	40	60	65	70	75
AFR	11	13	9	11	9
EAP	4	11	12	12	10
ECA[b]	9	16	16	16	22
LCR	8	8	12	11	16
MNA	2	7	6	8	8
SAR	6	5	10	12	10

a. Weighted average to account for oversampling of costlier tasks.

b. Includes four tasks in Turkey.

Source: World Bank data.

Table A.14 IFC Activites in Transition Countries, FY90–03

A: IFC Approvals and Net Commitments by Country, FY90–03

Transition Region/country	IFC gross approvals						IFC net approvals				IFC net commitments			
	By number			By volume			By number		By volume		By number		By volume	
	No. of projects	Percent of all transition	Including B-loans	Approvals (US$M)	Percent of all transition	Including B-loans	No. of projects	Percent of all transition	Approvals (US$M)	Percent of all transition	No. of projects	Percent of all transition	Sub-total	Percent of all transition
Central Europe														
Albania	12	2.8	2	227	2.8	64	12	2.8	163	2.8	4	1.1	33	0.9
Bosnia	16	3.7	2	100	1.2	8	16	3.7	92	1.6	18	5.0	70	2.0
Bulgaria	20	4.6	4	318	3.9	72	20	4.6	246	4.2	19	5.3	190	5.4
Croatia	14	3.2	4	219	2.7	48	14	3.2	171	2.9	13	3.6	144	4.1
Czech Republic	20	4.6	5	1,065	13.1	530	20	4.6	535	9.1	18	5.0	379	10.7
Hungary	26	6.0	5	498	6.1	123	26	6.0	375	6.4	20	5.6	192	5.4
Macedonia	13	3.0	1	107	1.3	25	13	3.0	82	1.4	14	3.9	69	1.9
Poland	33	7.6	8	587	7.2	153	33	7.6	434	7.4	27	7.5	217	6.1
Romania	26	6.0	7	633	7.8	240	25	5.8	393	6.7	24	6.7	252	7.1
Slovak Republic	9	2.1	1	159	2.0	3	9	2.1	156	2.7	5	1.4	55	1.5
Slovenia	6	1.4	2	33	0.4	8	6	1.4	24	0.4	5	1.4	19	0.5
Subtotal, Central Europe	195	45	41	3,945	49	1,274	194	45	2,671	46	167	47	1,619	46
FSU & Russia														
Armenia	3	0.7	0	11	0.1	0	3	0.7	11	0.2	2	0.6	6	0.2
Azerbaijan	13	3.0	1	245	3.0	100	13	3.0	145	2.5	15	4.2	136	3.9
Belarus	2	0.5	0	16	0.2	0	2	0.5	16	0.3	1	0.3	14	0.4
Georgia	13	3.0	0	74	0.9	0	13	3.0	74	1.3	14	3.9	65	1.8
Kazakhstan	33	7.6	7	762	9.4	272	32	7.4	490	8.4	22	6.1	263	7.4
Kyrgyz Republic	9	2.1	1	50	0.6	2	9	2.1	48	0.8	6	1.7	46	1.3
Moldova	6	1.4	1	89	1.1	25	6	1.4	64	1.1	11	3.1	60	1.7
Russia	87	20.0	14	2,141	26.4	393	86	19.9	1,749	29.8	64	17.8	984	27.9
Tajikistan	11	2.5	0	29	0.4	0	11	2.5	29	0.5	10	2.8	32	0.9
Turkmenistan	2	0.5	0	3	0.0	0	2	0.5	3	0.0	0	0.0	0	0.0
Ukraine	8	1.8	0	67	0.8	0	8	1.9	67	1.1	6	1.7	26	0.7
Uzbekistan	22	5.1	5	257	3.2	102	22	5.1	155	2.6	14	3.9	46	1.3
Subtotal, FSU & Russia	209	48	29	3,745	46	893	207	48	2,851	49	165	46	1,676	47
Baltics														
Estonia	16	3.7	1	154	1.9	9	16	3.7	145	2.5	17	4.7	129	3.7
Latvia	6	1.4	2	116	1.4	45	6	1.4	71	1.2	5	1.4	51	1.5
Lithuania	9	2.1	2	149	1.8	19	9	2.1	130	2.2	5	1.4	58	1.6
Subtotal, Baltics	31	7	5	420	5	74	31	7	346	6	27	8	239	7
Total transition	435	100	75	8,109	100	2,241	432	100	5,868	100	359	100	3,534	100
Total IFC	3,075	100	718	70,526	100	29,065	3,075	100	42,951	100	2,434	100	26,594	100
Transition as % of IFC	14.1		10.4	11.5		7.7	14		13.7		14.7		13.3	

Sources: OEG: Approval data are from BMS. Approved loans include guarantee amounts. Commitment data are from IFC, June 30, 2003. Net commitments are net of cancellation amounts.

ANNEX A: SUPPLEMENTARY TABLES

Table A.14	IFC Activites in Transition Countries, FY90–03 (continued)

B: IFC Technical Assistance, FY90–03

Transition Region/ country	Donor-funded TA (including TATF) By volume		Private Sector Advisory Services in Policy Transactions (PSAPT) By volume		Foreign Investment Advisory Service (FIAS) By number	
	Approvals (US$M)	Percent of all transition	Approvals (US$M)	Percent of all transition	No. of projects	Percent of all transition
Central Europe						
Albania	415,370	0	—	—	3	3
Bosnia	4,735,400	3	—	—	4	4
Bulgaria	822,000	1	77,777	1	7	7
Croatia	965,510	1	—	—	7	7
Czech Republic	1,976,000	1	2,668,262	20	4	4
Hungary	1,613,600	1	62,630	0	4	4
Macedonia	1,407,460	1	—	—	3	3
Poland	1,635,000	1	3,687,916	27	1	1
Romania	4,489,300	3	3,877,495	29	7	7
Slovak Republic	332,029	0	—	—	3	3
Slovenia	52,700	0	312,363	2	3	3
Regional (including SEED)	12,745,000	8	—	—	—	—
Subtotal, Central Europe	**30,685,369**	**20**	**10,686,442**	**79**	**46**	**44**
FSU & Russia						
Armenia	1,064,670	1	214,980	2	6	6
Azerbaijan	966,160	1	—	—	2	2
Belarus	8,890,000	6	—	—	1	1
Georgia	824,850	1	571,528	4	5	5
Kazakhstan	913,000	1	28,008	0	3	3
Kyrgyz Republic	643,980	0	—	—	7	7
Moldova	1,802,970	1	—	—	2	2
Russia	56,758,430	36	521,259	4	10	10
Tajikistan	3,325,860	2	—	—	—	—
Turkmenistan	60,000	0	—	—	—	—
Ukraine	39,637,379	25	1,441,511	11	2	2
Uzbekistan	1,404,900	1	—	—	1	1
Regional[a]	2,559,000	2	—	—	—	—
Subtotal, FSU & Russia	**118,851,199**	**76**	**2,777,286**	**21**	**39**	**38**
Baltics						
Estonia	600,000	0	—	—	3	3
Latvia	327,500	0	—	—	7	7
Lithuania	1,349,150	1	—	—	3	3
Regional	1,547,500	1	—	—	—	—
Subtotal, Baltics	**3,824,150**	**2**	**—**	**—**	**13**	**13**
Europe, regional	3,940,389	2	—	—	2	2
Total transition	**157,301,107**	**100**	**13,463,728**	**100**	**104**	**100**

a. Amounts raised through Private Enterprise Partnerships (PEPs) since FY01, totalling US$29 million, are distributed among individual PEP client countries.

Source: OEG.

Table A.15	MIGA Guarantees by Country, FY90–02					
Country	Projects	Contracts issued	Maximum aggregate liability (US$ thousands)	Country (% of total)	FDI facilitated (US$ thousands)	Country (% of total)
Albania	2	2	8,585	0.42	10,700	0.21
Armenia	1	1	2,700	0.13	3,000	0.06
Azerbaijan	3	5	74,888	3.63	59,455	1.18
Bosnia and Herzegovina	7	20	96,391	4.67	62,676	1.24
Bulgaria	7	10	70,005	3.39	979,317	19.43
Croatia	2	3	75,712	3.67	68,285	1.36
Czech Republic	6	10	232,276	11.26	537,966	10.68
Georgia	1	1	3,402	0.16	2,130	0.04
Hungary	5	9	70,644	3.42	199,304	3.96
Kazakhstan	5	10	66,169	3.21	135,582	2.69
Kyrgyz Republic	3	7	109,980	5.33	360,089	7.15
Macedonia	1	1	19,164	0.93	30,740	0.61
Moldova	2	2	63,792	3.09	139,000	2.76
Poland	9	12	146,398	7.09	486,660	9.66
Romania	6	9	207,255	10.04	215,206	4.27
Russian Federation	20	30	617,538	29.93	1,353,672	26.86
Slovak Republic	4	8	91,565	4.44	201,474	4.00
Turkmenistan	1	1	8,000	0.39	13,800	0.27
Ukraine	2	2	49,000	2.37	70,000	1.39
Uzbekistan	1	2	50,000	2.42	110,000	2.18
Total	**88**	**143**	**2,063,464**	100.00	**5,039,056**	100.00
Total overall MIGA guarantees, FY90–02	**376**	**597**	**11,056,000**		**45,822,247**	
Transition country (%)	**23.4**	**24.0**	**18.7**		**11.0**	

Source: OEU, MIGA.

Lesson	Recent CASs
ESW: Need more analytical work, especially Poverty Assessments (PAs) and Public Expenditure Reviews (PERs). Good Living Standards Measurement Study needed.	CASs emphasize core ESW.
Emphasize dissemination (inadequate in Poland, Bulgaria).	Do not discuss dissemination or strategy to achieve impact on authorities.
Sequence properly.	Not done: big loans do not always follow important ESW (e.g., social sector work in Bosnia and Herzegovina, Azerbaijan; PER in Albania done *after* major Structural Adjustment Credit dealing with public administration reform).
	ESW *was* properly sequenced in Armenia.
Build domestic capacity.	ESW as tool to build domestic capacity not discussed.
Participation: Consult with stakeholders, explain to population how Bank strategy tries to alleviate poverty.	Most CASs, especially from 2000+, developed in consultation. Client surveys/consultations show Bank has not yet been able to convincingly explain how the strategy will alleviate poverty.
Aid Coordination: Examine IMF role and show transparently in the CAS the areas supported by IMF, other donors, Bank.	All CASs discuss aid coordination. IMF role not highlighted.
Need to encourage govt. management of aid coordination.	No discussion of this in CASs.
Lending Instruments, Project Design: Build ownership for investment lending by improving relevance and efficacy and developing project prioritization skills.	CASs discuss portfolio performance, lessons, but do not discuss how to improve relevance of projects.
Take better account of country-level relevance in components of investment projects (Kazakhstan urban transport, Bulgaria health financed low-priority investments).	CASs do not discuss allocation of investments within projects.
Risk Assessment: Need more realism in assessing progress, risks, government commitment.	Most CASs have very good discussion of risk to the Bank, especially Russia, Ukraine, Romania. Very transparent
Need to improve contingency planning for risky countries (Kyrgyz).	about lack of political support for reform. Risk mitigation strategy is defined solely in terms of lending volumes.

Lesson	Recent CASs
In projects avoid broad Structural Adjustment Loans (SALs) if uncertain commitment; use floating tranches, Sectoral Adjustment Loans (SECALs) instead of SALs.	Lending scenarios avoid SALs when uncertain commitment; they do not suggest floating tranches or SECALs.
Selectivity, Comparative Advantage: In choosing sectors for Bank lending, look at subsectors as well (e.g., other donors active in transport, but Bank could have financed rural roads; other donors active in education, so Bank stayed out, but not clear what others doing).	All CASs say Bank will be selective, according to comparative advantage, but basically a list of where other donors involved. Underlying theme is that Bank will stay out of infrastructure because other donors supporting it, but not clear if all subsectors relevant to constraints are covered.
	Good discussion of comparative advantage in Slovenia, Kazakhstan, Kyrgyz, Hungary.
Capacity Building: Need to develop capacity for monitoring and evaluation and for donor coordination.	No discussion in any CAS of strategy to build domestic capacity for either area
Monitorability of CAS: CAS benchmarks should be monitorable.	Performance monitoring a separate section in most CASs. But indicators are not monitorable (e.g., reduction, steady improvement, continued progress).
	Very well done in Slovak Rep., Armenia, Kazakhstan.
Need to say how will identify turning points in a country's performance (for poor performers).	CASs for Turkmenistan, Belarus say no new loans unless policy performance improves. Belarus shifts focus to ESW, supervision. But monitoring system to identify turning points is not evident.
Governance, Legal Reform, Institutions: Bank has paid insufficient attention to these areas. They are key to EU accession, and they are binding constraints in non-EU countries.	CASs have substantial focus on governance, and greater attention than earlier to legal reform.
Focus on broader governance and accountability arrangements, not narrowly on PSM.	CASs are focusing on broader governance issues, but not clear what and where the weaknesses are in accountability arrangements. The discussion across countries is virtually indistinguishable in diagnosis.
Need more balance between PSM and PSD.	CASs have very balanced discussion of PSM, PSD.
Poverty, Gender: Need greater government commitment to poverty alleviation, particularly in targeting social assistance to the vulnerable.	Govt. commitment to poverty alleviation is assumed, except Kazakhstan, where a difference between government and Bank is noted.
	Link between poverty reduction and proposed actions is not stated.
	No discussion of potential social impact of policy reforms.
	Social protection discussion more extensive than health, education.
Use existing work to inform design of projects on gender.	No statement of which projects will mainstream gender.
Design should include poverty identification and targeting.	

Lesson	Recent CASs
Decentralization: Need more advice on decentralization issues (Kazakhstan, Bulgaria devolved responsibility for social assistance to local governments, but it became a residual in the budget and exacerbated inter-regional inequalities).	Rarely discussed.
Privatization, PSD: Need more work on enabling environment, governance, legal and regulatory framework and its enforcement, judicial reform, transparency in privatization, reduction in arbitrary tax laws.	CASs acknowledge that enforcement of laws and regulations is weak and the judiciary ineffective, but the strategy to deal with these issues is not clear.
Mass privatization only for small enterprises; auction approach in environment of weak corporate governance led to asset stripping. Don't encourage management employee buyouts (MEBOs) (e.g., Bulgaria). Address fiscal aspects of privatization. Trying to restructure large SOEs without strategic investor involvement rarely works.	Little discussion of privatization methods. No discussion of corporate governance.
Use full range of Bank Group instruments—IFC, MIGA, Bank.	CASs describe what IFC, MIGA and Bank are doing, and have generic statements of how these activities complement each other, but no specifics on how the three will work together in specific PSD areas.
Apply lessons from IFC, MIGA experience.	Results from PSD surveys, client surveys are noted, but nothing on actual transaction experiences of IFC, MIGA.
Financial Sector: Needs greater attention.	CASs give attention to financial sector.
Avoid directed credit.	No CAS suggests directed credit.
Agriculture: Needs greater attention.	Receiving more attention.
Where vested interests dominate (Ukraine), with monopsonistic/monopolistic powers, no adjustment lending. Focus on locally based integrated farm support projects. Beware privatization projects that lead to very small holdings.	Vested interests dominate in a number of transition economies, and adjustment lending is still given.
Infrastructure: Work with government to set up infrastructure privatization program and related regulatory framework. Do not work with dysfunctional public utilities. Need fundamental change in management, employee incentives, accountability structures.	CASs emphasize regulatory frameworks before privatization. Stopped working with dysfunctional public utilities in early 1990s. CASs discuss public administration reform, but not resource based management or accountability.
Energy: Needs greater attention, especially to get prices right. Persuade authorities that power sector needs to operate independently and commercially.	
Education:	Relatively neglected.

Source: ECA Region CASs and OED CAEs.

ANNEX C:·· PEOPLE INTERVIEWED[1]

Asad Alam	Lead Economist, Poverty Reduction and Economic Management (ECSPE)
James Anderson	Economist, Poverty Reduction and Economic Management (ECSPE)
Robert J. Anderson	Former Lead Economist, ECAVP
Emily Andrews	Lead Economist (ECSHD)
Laura Ard	Lead Financial Sector Specialist, Financial Sector Operations and Policy Department (OPD)
Asad Alam	Sector Manager (ECSPE)
Konstantin Atanesyan	Consultant (ECSPE)
Marie Bakker	Lead Financial Sector Specialist, Private & Financial Sectors Development Sector Unit (ECSPF)
Luca Barbone	Country Director, Belarus, Moldova, Ukraine
Sandra Bloemenkamp	Senior Public Sector Management Specialist (ECSPE)
Lilia Burunciuc	Country Program Coordinator, Central Asia Country Unit (ECCU8)
Henk Busz	Sector Manager, Energy Unit, Europe and Central Asia Regional Office
David Craig	Country Director, Burkina Faso, Mali, Mauritania, São Tomé and Príncipe, (AFC15)
Maria Dakolias	Lead Counsel, Legal and Judicial Reform Unit (LEGLR)
John Eriksson	Consultant, Corporate Evaluations and Methods (OEDCM)
Gabriella Ferencz	Lead Financial Sector Specialist (OPD)
Gary Fine	Senior Private Sector Development Specialist, Private & Financial Sectors Development Sector Unit (ECSPF)
Alexander Fleming	Sector Manager, Finance and Private Sector Development, World Bank Institute (WBIFP)
Louse Fox	Lead Specialist (AFTPM)
Michael Fuchs	Lead Financial Specialist, Financial Sector Unit, Africa, Africa Technical Families (AFTFS)
Kathryn Funk	Country Officer, Albania
Prem Garg	Director, Quality Assurance Group (QAG)
Jit Bahadur Gill	Lead Public Sector Management Specialist (ECSPE)
Roger Grawe	Country Director, Czech Republic, Hungary, Moldova, Slovak Republic, Slovenia
Cheryl Gray	Sector Director (ECSPE)
Poonam Gupta	Senior Evaluation Officer, Country Evaluation and Regional Relations (OEDCR)
Sanjeev Gupta	Assistant Director, Fiscal Affairs Department, IMF
John Hegarty	Manager, Operations Policy and Services (ECSPS)
Joel Hellman	Senior Public Management Specialist (ECSPE)
Jane Holt	Sector Manager, Environment (ECSSD)

Elliot Hurwitz	Consultant, Country Evaluation and Regional Relations (OEDCR)
Alma Kanani	Senior Economist (ECSPE)
Basil Kavalsky	Former Country Director, Armenia, Belarus, Estonia, Georgia, Latvia, Lithuania, Moldova, Poland, Ukraine
Philip Keefer	Lead Economist, Development Research Group (DECRG)
Ioannis Kessides	Lead Economist, Development Research Group (DECRG)
Hoonae Kim	Sector Manager, Rural Development, East Asia & Pacific Regional Office (EASRD)
Jeni Klugman	Lead Economist, Poverty Reduction Group (PREMPR)
Peter Kyle	Lead Counsel, Private Sector Development, Finance, and Infrastructure (LEGPS)
Geoffrey Lamb	Director, Resource Mobilization Department (FRM)
Michael Lav	Consultant, Country Evaluation and Regional Relations (OEDCR)
Ira Lieberman	Senior Policy Adviser, Private & Financial Sectors Development Sector Units, Europe and Central Asia Regional Office (ECSPF)
Robert Liebenthal	Former Manager (ECHSD)
David Lindeman	Consultant
Johannes Linn	Regional Vice President, Europe and Central Asia (ECAVP)
Robert Liu	Adviser (OPD)
Laszlo Lovei	Economic Advisor, Delivery Management, Operations Policy and Country Services (OPCDM)
Alexandre Marc	Sector Manager, Environmentally and Socially Sustainable Development Unit
Albert Martinez	Lead Private Sector Development Specialist, Quality Assurance Group (QAG)
Kathleen McCollom	Chief Administrative Officer (ECA)
Rick Messick	Senior Public Sector Specialist, Public Sector Management Division (PRMPS)
Michael Mills	Lead Economist (ECSHD)
Pradeep Mitra	Chief Economist (ECA)
Allister Moon	Lead Economist (ECSPE)
Helga Muller	Sector Manager (ECSPE)
Craig Neal	Senior Public Sector Specialist (ECSPE)
John Nellis	Senior Fellow, Center for Global Development (Former World Bank Staff, PSD)
Judy O'Connor	Former Country Director, Georgia
Neil Parison	Senior Public Sector Management Specialist (ECSPE)
Kyle Peters	Senior Manager, Country Evaluation and Regional Relations (OEDCR)
Christiaan Poortman	Former Country Director, Albania, Bosnia and Herzegovina, Macedonia, Serbia
Sanjay Pradhan	Sector Director (PRMPS)
Svetlana Proskurovska	Public Sector Management Specialist (ECSPE)
Mansoora Rashid	Sector Manager (SASHD)
Gary Reid	Lead Public Sector Management Specialist (ECSPE)
Roberto Rocha	Lead Financial Sector Economist (OPD)
Michal Rutkowski	Manager (ECSHD)
Randi Ryterman	Sector Manager, Public Sector Management Division, Poverty Reduction and Economic Management Network (PRMPS)
Gerald Saunders	Deputy Legal Counsel, EBRD

Hjalte Sederlof	Consultant (ECSHD)
Paul Siegelbaum	Former Director, Private & Financial Sectors Development Sector Unit (ECSPF)
Sander Sipos	Sector Manager, Social Protection (HDNSP)
Martin Slough	Senior Financial Specialist, Private & Financial Sectors Development Sector Unit (ECSPF)
John Spears	Consultant, Environment Department (ENV)
Gary Stuggins	Lead Energy Economist, Energy Unit, Energy and Water Department
Helen Sutch	Sector Manager (PRMPS)
Peter Thomson	Sector Manager, Energy Unit, Europe and Central Regional Office (ECSIE)
Tunc Uyanik	Sector Manager, Financial Sector Unit (ECSPF)
Herman von Gersdorff	Lead Economist (ECSHD)
Deborah Wetzel	Sector Manager, Macroeconomics (ECSPE)
Suzy Yoon	Operations Officer, Delivery Management (OPCDM)

Interviewed Earlier by Transition Evaluation Team in Context of Russia CAE

William Alexander	IMF
Anastossia Alexandrova	Consultant (ECCU1)
Lajos Bokros	Director, Financial Advisory Services (ECAVP)
Jeanine Braithwaite	Senior Economist (ECSHD)
Cesare Calari	Vice President and Head of Network, Financial Sector Vice Presidency (FSEVP)
Russell J. Cheetham	Former Country Director, Russia
Michael Carter	Country Director, India
Walter Cohn	Consultant, IFC, OEG
Kathryn Dahlmeier	Social Protection Specialist (ECSHD)
Ruben Lamdany	Director, Sector and Thematic Program, World Bank Institute (WBIST)
Ken Lay	Deputy Treasurer and Director, Banking, Capital Markets & Financial Engineering Department (BCF)
Andrei Markov	Senior Human Development Specialist (ECSHD)
Gerhard Pohl	Consultant, Informatics Program (ISGIF)
Nicholas Stern	Former Chief Economist, EBRD and IBRD
Jacques Toureille	Lead Financial Sector Specialist, Staff Exchange Program (PA9ES)
Elena Zotova	Senior Technical Specialist (ECSHD)

Introduction

Management welcomes the review by the Operations Evaluation Department (OED) of World Bank assistance to the transition economies. As OED notes, this is a meta-evaluation, which is largely based on previous evaluative work. Like other evaluative work, it uses the benefit of 20/20 hindsight. The review assesses the effectiveness of World Bank assistance to the transition countries in the Europe and Central Asia Region (ECA), with a view to eliciting lessons for countries undergoing similar, if less extreme, changes in the future.

OED Findings

The report concludes that the countries of the Region have achieved substantial overall progress. The private sector share of gross domestic product across all transition countries, virtually nil in 1989, reached nearly 70 percent in 2002, even including the late-starting post-conflict Southeast European countries and the most reluctant reformers. Eight Central and Eastern European and Baltic countries joined the European Union on May 1, 2004, and others are expected to join in the next several years. Furthermore, policy reform has progressed steadily in most countries, with few reversals.

World Bank Support. The World Bank, in collaboration with the IMF, the European Union, and other donors, geared up rapidly to support macroeconomic stabilization and structural reform and, later, to provide post-conflict support in Southeastern Europe, in particular. The report notes that the Bank's strategy was to promote macroeconomic stability and sound economic management, reorient and strengthen public sector institutions, build the basic institutions of

a market economy and an enabling environment for private sector initiatives, and cushion the social cost of the transition. It considers these objectives to be relevant and concludes that the Bank's assistance to the transition countries was on the whole successful. In assessing the effectiveness of such assistance, OED recognizes that the collapse of the Soviet Union and the ensuing transition took place with little warning and on an unparalleled scale. The report mentions that political imperatives put the Bank under pressure to move quickly and lend large amounts, and that staff were frequently confronted with the need to act, often under difficult circumstances, with no relevant experience and little country knowledge, learning along the way. It also recognizes that the Bank's role, though small relative to overall financial flows—except in a few small countries—was significant in terms of analytical work and policy advice.

The Report's View of the Shortcomings of Bank Support, with Hindsight. The report argues that clearly there were mistakes early on when the true nature of transition was not yet fully understood, and that the effectiveness of the initial strategy was limited because (a) the Bank underestimated the need to focus systematically on poverty alleviation and good governance, and (b) its use of rapid privatization to promote private sector development did not always achieve its intended effect without a supporting legal and institutional framework. Over time, the Bank is seen as having internalized emerging lessons and having shifted its emphasis accordingly: poverty alleviation, monitoring, and good governance are now prominent objectives in both lending and analytic work, and the approach to privatization and private sector development has evolved considerably. The report also takes the view, again with the benefit of hindsight, that more prudent lending levels would have been better in the long run for those low-income Commonwealth of Independent States (CIS) countries—where the transitional recession was far deeper and longer than originally foreseen and where problems of governance were more serious than anticipated—that which now face significant levels of indebtedness.

Recommendations. The report concludes with three recommendations for the Bank: (a) promote ownership and consensus, (b) improve the effectiveness of its instruments, and (c) define clear strategies for assistance—differentiated by the state of governance and institutional capacity in borrowing countries—in the following areas: legal and judicial reform; energy sector enterprise reform; privatization; pension reform; and transparency and accountability, including through wide dissemination of its own studies. Management is in general agreement with the thrust of these recommendations. Details are provided in the Management Action Record, attached as an annex to this Management Response.

Management Comments

The issues highlighted by the OED report are undeniably better understood in retrospect. The pace of change was so tumultuous, particularly in the early years of transition, that the information available with perfect hindsight is necessarily very different from that available earlier, a consideration that limits the applicability of the lessons OED seeks to draw as a guide to action in countries undergoing similar, if less extreme, changes. Inasmuch as future actors in such situations must base policies on information available ex ante, it would have been useful to evaluate whether the Bank made the best use of knowledge available at the time; how well its processes balanced the need to draw on a range of diverse opinions with the need for timely intervention in crisis-like situations; and how it responded to pressures from major shareholders, clients, and other constituencies. At the same time, the evaluation provides a thoughtful contribution to the

analysis of this unique experience. As the report indicates, the Bank has internalized and acted on the emerging lessons coming from its experience in supporting transition economies, notably with regard to poverty, support for private sector development, and governance.

An Unprecedented Event in History. The transition in Eastern Europe and the former Soviet Union was a seminal event, involving political, social, and economic transformation on an unprecedented scale. No one working on the transition economies, whether in the Bank or outside it, foresaw the depth and severity of the transition recession in the CIS countries. The report acknowledges the relatively short and shallow recession in Central Europe, which had been broadly foreseen. The expectation of a comparably short and shallow recession in the CIS, held by many, including the Bank's key counterparts, combined with the fact of low poverty and inequality in the Region to start with, implied that any increase in poverty would be transitional. Thus an emphasis on poverty alleviation would have been misplaced. The Bank therefore focused on alleviating transitional poverty to the extent tight budgetary realities would permit, by protecting pensions because the elderly were at risk, and on retargeting social assistance to those affected by downsizing of enterprises rendered unviable following price liberalization. It must also be noted that governments in transition countries during the early years were reluctant to accept the notion of social assistance, possibly because of the enduring stigma of poverty, and to borrow for that purpose from institutions associated with developing countries. In this context, clients would not have been receptive to a stronger Bank emphasis on poverty alleviation. Later, when it became clear that the recession was deeper and more severe than originally expected, the Bank focused its programs more strongly on poverty reduction. In the realm of analytic work, the Region took the lead in publishing a landmark study on poverty and inequality in Europe and Central Asia (World Bank 2000c; at the same time as the World Development Report 2000/2001 on poverty, World Bank 2000e), which has been influential in sensitizing the development community to poverty and inequality issues across transition countries. Indeed, as the OED report notes, reflecting this evolution, poverty alleviation is now prominent in the Region's lending and analytic work, along with support for growth.

The Prevailing Environment in the Early Years of Transition. The observation that the Bank's strategy was mistaken because it paid little attention to good governance in the early years of transition could usefully take more fully into account the environment prevailing in the countries of the Region at that time. The Bank's assistance program started amid massive uncertainty and real concerns, especially in the CIS, as to whether the old, highly repressive regime might come back to power or enterprises might be grabbed by local governments—more broadly, whether the irreversibility of steps toward a market economy was guaranteed. In 1991, for example, President Yeltsin mounted a tank to stop an insurrection by the communists in Russia. The fluidity of these situations called for speed on the part of the reformers and the Bank and, as a practical matter, precluded the luxury of taking a significant amount of time to analyze governance and public sector management issues. Nevertheless, the Bank's programs worked to depoliticize the allocation of resources through price and trade liberalization and through a more transparent budget process to make explicit the myriad of implicit subsidies and greater transparency in the tax system. It also needs to be remembered that the Bank started developing its strategy on anticorruption and good governance in the mid-1990s; these issues were to become explicit institutional priorities only later in the decade when the analytic toolkits for addressing them were developed. When this internal shift occurred, ECA's efforts to operationalize these policies placed it at the forefront among the Bank's Regions.

Administrative Structure and Public Institutions. In a similar vein, the report observes that while the Bank understood the need to reorient and strengthen public sector institutions, it greatly underestimated the consequences of still weak core institutions and public administrations managing the transition process. The Region's own

retrospective (World Bank 2002b) on transition acknowledges that, while developing market-compatible institutions had been on the reform agenda since the onset of transition, the challenge of doing so in countries without recent market experience was underestimated. OED also believes that the Bank often approached public sector management reform in an ad hoc manner, without a comprehensive, long-term institutional development and reform strategy. But the report may overstate its case in saying that little analysis of public expenditures was undertaken before the late 1990s. Although stand-alone Public Expenditure Reviews were relatively rare in ECA and throughout the Bank, many public sector interventions in ECA were preceded by analytic work on public expenditure in Country Economic Memoranda or sector reports carried out in the earlier part of the decade.

Emphasis on Privatization. The report questions the relevance of Bank strategy in the early years because of its heavy emphasis on privatization to achieve private sector development in countries where institutions of corporate governance were not in place, thus risking the expropriation of minority shareholders' assets and income of those who had gained control over the enterprise. Since privatization of small enterprises is widely regarded as having been highly successful, this is a critique of privatization of medium and large enterprises. But the report does not mention that the alternative of delaying privatization of medium- and large-scale enterprises until institutions of corporate governance had begun to function was extremely problematic as well. It would have left enterprise assets in the hands of enterprise managers where state authority had collapsed, leaving the state in the hands of a self-serving and corrupt nomenklatura and intensifying the use of asset stripping and other forms of capture. Hence, except in situations where there was a strategic investor to whom assets could be directly sold, policymakers were faced with an extremely difficult choice between two unattractive alternatives. Indeed, it is not clear now, even with the benefit of perfect hindsight, which of these would have been the preferred course of action. The fact that—as

OED notes in its report—there have been no significant policy reversals in the transition countries, except in those that have not substantially embarked on market reforms, is a remarkable achievement and must owe something to the reformers' strategy of creating a new and evidently irreversible economic reality through rapid and early privatization. This is a complex and controversial area, and not enough time has elapsed to allow a considered judgment to be made.

Second-Generation Reforms. On a related note, the report observes that, in line with views of leading policymakers throughout the Region, early Bank assistance put a lower priority on reform of regulatory, antimonopoly, commercial, capital market, and bankruptcy regimes—the so-called "second generation" reforms—leaving them to be pursued once a critical mass of privatized firms had appeared.[1] It takes the view that in the earliest years of the transition, many of the Bank's choices were probably appropriate, given what was known at the time. This position might seem to be at odds with the report's criticism of the Bank's emphasis on privatization, a criticism that is based on hindsight, illustrating the difficulty of making some kinds of judgments in an environment of rapidly changing information. However, with the benefit of hindsight, the report also considers that the Bank should have been quicker to pursue the lessons drawn by the Region in its retrospective, which are noted as being consistent with OED's findings. It goes on to say that by the mid-1990s it is reasonable to ask whether the Bank was focusing sufficiently on the climate for private sector development and the appropriate methods for disciplining and privatizing medium and large enterprises.

The Lessons from the Region's Retrospective. The lessons from the retrospective that are relevant with regard to this issue call for (a) privatization as part of a broad strategy of discipline (imposing hard budget constraints on enterprises and banks and monitoring managerial behavior) and encouragement (a business environment that levels the playing field among state-owned, privatized, and de novo firms); (b) quick sale of small enterprises through open and competitive auctions;

(c) case-by-case privatization of medium and large enterprises; (d) an enforceable legal system to protect investors; (e) increased competition; (f) clarification of the cash flow and property rights of enterprises with continued state ownership; and (g) an efficient regulatory regime before divestiture of enterprises in sectors characterized by natural monopoly or oligopoly. However, understanding the context in which these lessons were drawn is of the utmost importance.

The Context for Learning the Lessons on the Private Sector in Transition Economies. There are two relevant points to be made. First, as already noted, the need to create an irreversible economic reality often dictated rapid privatization in the early years, when the return of Communism was felt to be an ever-present danger in the CIS countries. But once that threat had receded over time, it was appropriate for the Region's retrospective, drawing on 10 years of country experience, to advocate taking a more nuanced approach to privatization in the context of a strategy of discipline and encouragement. That said, the Bank should have critiqued poor privatization decisions, such as the loans-for-shares scheme in Russia, and expressed its reservations regarding mass privatization using vouchers in Bosnia in the mid-1990s. Second, a greater emphasis on entry and expansion of de novo firms ("the new private sector"), which have played an important role in economic recovery and job creation in conjunction with privatization and restructuring, would have been appropriate in the mid-1990s. However, it must be noted that it was not until the Region's retrospective was written that the development community fully understood the mutual complementarity of entry and expansion of de novo firms on the one hand and privatization and restructuring on the other, so that neither could proceed very far without the other.

Initial Conditions and Policy Response Lags. The report's assessment of the early years of transition could set the developments of those years in a broader context. The literature on initial conditions, policy reform, and outcomes makes clear that, when initial conditions are controlled for, countries that implemented policy reforms witnessed a favorable impact on output growth over the medium term. This importantly implies that the favorable outcomes noted in the later part of the period under review owe something to the reforms undertaken in the early years of transition and, therefore, that an assessment of the Bank's assistance in the early years cannot be undertaken by looking solely at outcomes in those years.

Debt Sustainability in CIS Countries. The report argues, again with the benefit of hindsight, that more prudent lending levels would have been better in the low-income CIS countries, which are now significantly indebted. The report notes that this was because official lending levels were based on the ex ante expectation that the transition recession in the CIS countries would be short and shallow. This issue has been examined in the context of the CIS 7 Initiative that the Bank and the IMF have undertaken, in conjunction with the European Bank for Reconstruction and Development and the Asian Development Bank (see http://www.cis7.org). As already noted, neither the international financial institutions (IFIs) nor other observers foresaw the extent of disruption arising from the dissolution of the Soviet Union. In the event, financing of the initial transition by the IFIs and other donors prevented a further compression of living standards in countries where they were already in precipitous decline. Hence OED's view that less lending would have been better implies that such a further compression—in countries that were undergoing significant adjustment—and the resulting lower debt would have been preferable to the situation that prevails today. The trade-off between cushioning the fall in living standards and ensuring debt sustainability would have been moderated if more grant financing had been forthcoming in the early years, which could then have been followed by Bank (and other IFI) financing to support structural reform. This raises the question of whether more efforts should have been made to secure grant financing for the low-income CIS countries in those years. However, it also needs to be pointed out that substantial and steady growth in the low-income CIS countries since 2000, together with debt relief granted by official creditors, has played a major role in reducing their debt burden since 2001.

OED Recommendations. As OED notes, its findings and recommendations are broadly applicable across World Bank support for most countries. All of the recommendations on sectoral issues—legal and judicial reform, financial sector lending, energy sector reform priorities and sequencing, support for privatization, and advice on pension reform—are useful and timely. The cross-sectoral findings—importance of a knowledge base and relevant and timely economic and sector work; the promotion of government ownership and leadership on aid coordination; a comprehensive, long-term approach to public sector management reform and institution-building; and the high priority of poverty monitoring—are of relevance for ongoing work on Bank support to client countries. Detailed responses to OED's specific recommendations are attached in the Management Action Record.

Conclusions

Bank Management welcomes the OED review of Bank support to transition economies and the opportunity to discuss and contrast its own self-evaluation of this unique experience with the views of OED. While the recommendations are generic and not particularly related to transition economies, Management finds them intuitive and accepts them, with a few small qualifications. As noted above, Management believes that, while 20/20 hindsight is one approach, the report could have benefited from analysis that took more into account what was known about the transition economies at the time critical support decisions were taken. That type of analysis might have been more useful for informing the development community on how best to draw on available information and balance diverse views when going into a totally new environment and how to balance the need for timely financial support and learning by doing against the need for a solid analytic foundation. That said, Management thanks OED for a thoughtful review. As the report notes, the Bank has acted to incorporate the major lessons learned in its support to these transition economies.

Management Action Record

OED Recommendation	Management Response
1. The Bank should help promote ownership and consensus:	1. Management agrees with the recommendation that the Bank should promote ownership and consensus. That concept is at the heart of the Comprehensive Development Framework, which is now mainstreamed.
a. CASs should support capacity building for government and civil society, promote stakeholder participation, and take into account the underlying political and social processes that affect stakeholder behavior.	a. Management monitors CASs for the inclusion of support for capacity building. The current work on guidance on social development is addressing issues related to stakeholder analysis and participation. That work is planned for completion before the end of FY05. It should be noted, however, that Bank promotion of stakeholder participation must be done in the context of government ownership and leadership, supporting and encouraging country efforts, rather than trying to impose a system from the outside.
b. ESW should be undertaken with borrower participation and CASs should include a strategy for its dissemination.	b. Management encourages active borrower participation in most ESW tasks, particularly in core diagnostic ESW. In fact, QAG's assessments have demonstrated a growing trend in the share of participatory ESW. Regional as well as Sector Board guidelines emphasize the benefits of client participation in the preparation of diagnostic ESW products. Therefore, in most cases, client participation is expected. However, there will always be some cases in which clients are primarily interested in the Bank's own analyses and views, as that of a neutral, independent party. In these instances active borrower participation in the preparation of the report/policy note would be counterproductive. At Bankwide reviews of draft CASs, ESW programs, including issues of dissemination, are regularly part of the agenda. However, the CAS is already heavily loaded and Management does not intend to impose a new requirement with regard to a strategy for ESW dissemination.
2. The Bank should improve the effectiveness of its instruments:	2. Management agrees with the overall recommendation. The Bank works constantly to improve the effectiveness of its instruments and uses self- and independent evaluation to measure progress. Management would like to note that it does not agree with several of the separate recommendations embedded in the sub-recommendations, in particular one concerning analytic work as a prerequisite to sizeable lending. In general, this will be the case; but there are likely to be cases (notably in emergencies and turn-around situations) where Bank support that might be regarded as sizeable will have to proceed before or in parallel with analytic work.
a. Poverty levels should be monitored regularly, particularly in new borrowers.	a. This is Bank policy; however, in many cases there are issues of capacity that must be addressed with the support of the Bank or other donors, particularly in new borrowers.
b. Analytical work on governance and public sector management, along with analysis already required to understand the structure of	b. Three years ago, Management launched a systematic effort to strengthen the diagnostic underpinnings of Bank lending to clients with sizeable lending programs, particularly in the areas of public expenditure manage-

Management Action Record (*continued*)

OED Recommendation	Management Response
public expenditures and enhance public financial accountability, should precede sizeable lending.	ment, financial accountability, and procurement. The diagnostic instruments used by Bank staff (PER, CFAA, and CPAR) have evolved considerably since then, with increasing emphasis on governance issues. While additional analytic work dedicated specifically to governance and public sector management issues may be needed in some countries, Management believes that a formal requirement applied to all countries with planned lending operations above a certain size may lead to duplication of effort—in cases where sufficient knowledge can be gained from work undertaken/planned by partner agencies or local institutions—and can also crowd out traditional sector work essential to ensure high-quality investment lending.
c. The quality and impact of ESW should be evaluated retrospectively.	c. This is already the case. QAG undertook several rounds of ESW quality assessments in the FY98-03 period. Likely impact was one of the dimensions along which the quality of individual ESW products was assessed. Recognizing the limitations of this product-by-product impact evaluation methodology, QAG has moved to the quality review of entire ESW and (nonlending) TA programs in selected countries. These comprehensive country AAA assessments—one has been recently completed for Slovakia—have proven to be better suited to judge the impact of ESW. Management has also recognized that there is a need to improve the self-evaluation of individual ESW products and has developed a new very simple and cost effective results framework that will require ex ante the clear identification of the goals for each ESW task and ex post the evaluation of the extent to which these goals were achieved. This new framework will be implemented in SAP starting during FY05. In addition CAS Completion Reports look at the impact of ESW programs. If, as expected, CAS Completion Reports are mainstreamed, these reports and the related OED reviews will provide regular assessments of the impact of ESW at the appropriate level: the entire country ESW program over the CAS period.
d. Recipient governments should lead aid coordination, with donors helping them define clear development strategies, including monitorable action plans for implementation.	d. The PRSP process provides a framework in low-income countries for recipient governments to take the lead in aid coordination. Donors including the Bank help PRSP countries define clear development strategies with monitorable action plans for implementation. Regular Progress Reports by IMF and Bank staff measure progress.
3. The Bank should define clear strategies for assistance in the following areas, differentiated by the state of governance and institutional capacity of each country:	3. Management agrees in principle that clear strategies are important but does not agree with all of the details in the many complex recommendations that are imbedded in the overall recommendation and does not plan any new SSPs in the near future. Guidance to staff exists or is under preparation in each of these areas.

Management Action Record (*continued*)

OED Recommendation	Management Response
a. Legal and judicial reform, with a focus on implementation, is needed to improve the business climate (e.g., company, security, bankruptcy, and anti-monopoly laws, contractual rights, and respect for private property); the financial sector (banking, central banking, collateral, failed bank resolution); social protection (labor laws); and governance in general. Financial sector lending should be conditioned on progress in enforcing prudential regulations and international accounting standards, and in increasing the effectiveness of bank supervision.	a. The Legal Department and the Public Sector Governance Board of the PREM Network are working together on developing modes of support for both legal and judicial reform, in support of private sector development (and poverty reduction). Much of the guidance for supporting countries embarking on legal or judicial reform is summarized under Topics in Development on the Bank's external website under Law and Justice and also Public Sector Governance (Legal Institutions of the Market Economy). The Legal Department also maintains a list of qualified consultants in this field. Quality assurance with regard to financial sector lending, including on issues of effective prudential regulation, international accounting standards, and the effectiveness of Bank supervision is undertaken by the Financial Sector Network, based on the Board-endorsed Financial Sector Strategy.
b. The primary objectives for enterprises in the energy sector should be improved commercial performance and corporate governance; the sequencing of reforms, including the feasibility of immediate privatization, depends on country circumstances. Rehabilitation projects should minimize delays (use negative lists) and forego project implementation units and long-term reform objectives.	b. In response to the OED/OEG/OEU review, *Private Sector Development in the Electric Power Sector*, Management provided a guidance note to staff regarding the roles of the public and private sectors in the supply of electricity services. The note calls on staff who are providing advice to client countries to consider the full range of options, from purely public to purely private interventions. It notes that the course that power sector reform can take and the speed at which reforms can be implemented vary from country to country, and that reform is a continuous, evolving process. With regard to rehabilitation projects, negative lists may sometimes be appropriate. However, rehabilitation of capital stock often focuses on catching up on deferred maintenance and component replacement, requiring a detailed technical analysis followed by a targeted set of investments. It is not clear that using a negative list would be appropriate or would save time in these situations. Management agrees that long-term objectives should not be included in this type of investment loan and has made this clear to staff. As noted in the Management Response to the OED review of the CDF, Management is preparing a good practice note on PIUs and plans to have it available early FY05.
c. The emphasis in future privatizations should be on encouraging a carefully prepared, transparent, competitive process, open to foreign participation.	c. This is, in general, the kind of advice being given by Bank staff supporting privatization efforts. There is a large amount of information on this issue available within and outside the Bank. However, as in all Bank support, country conditions need to be taken into account, including on the issue of foreign participation.
d. A strategic approach is needed for pension reform and for improved targeting of social assistance programs other than pensions,	d. With regard to pension reform, the Social Protection Sector Board is producing a pensions position paper calling for an approach to Bank support that is both differentiated and strategic. The Social Protection

Management Action Record (*continued*)

OED Recommendation	Management Response
differentiated by the ability of the country to administer and fund the systems.	Strategy, now under implementation, calls for support for social assistance that is differentiated by the country's situation, priorities, and needs. The upcoming Sector Strategy Implementation Update will report on progress on all dimensions of the Social Protection Strategy, including these.
e. The Bank should promote transparency and accountability by ensuring that its own studies and documents are widely disseminated whenever possible, and by encouraging governments to report more regularly and more fully to their parliaments and to the public at large, including through information and communications technology.	e. Transparency and accountability are at the center of the Bank's Public Sector Management Strategy, under implementation. On the basis of that strategy, Bank support to governments emphasizes the importance of these issues, notably in the context of PERs, CFAAs, and CPARs. Within the Bank, recent revisions of the disclosure policy have significantly expanded the set of Bank documents that are made available regularly to the public. Further changes are under consideration by Executive Directors.

ANNEX E: CHAIRPERSON'S SUMMARY: COMMITTEE ON DEVELOPMENT EFFECTIVENESS (CODE)

On May 19, 2004, the Committee on Development Effectiveness (CODE) discussed the OED report entitled *An Evaluation of World Bank Assistance to the Transition Economies* together with the *Management Response to the OED Review*. Written statements were issued by three members.

Background. The OED study, undertaken in response to a request from CODE members, examined the effectiveness of World Bank assistance in 26 transition economies in the Europe and Central Asia Region (ECA) since 1989, with a view to eliciting lessons for countries undergoing similar, if less dramatic, changes in the future. Although the evaluation did not include all areas where the Bank was active, it provided an in-depth examination of five areas of Bank assistance: private sector development; governance, public sector management and institution building; financial sector; social protection; and energy. Overall, the OED report ranked Bank assistance to the transition countries as successful, but argued that there were mistakes early on when the true nature of transition was not fully understood. The report found the Bank's objectives relevant, but of limited effectiveness during the early years. The main reasons for that, according to the report, were an initial lack of focus on poverty and good governance and the use of rapid privatization to promote private sector development without a supporting legal and institutional framework. The report mentioned that the unexpectedly prolonged recession in some CIS countries led to the accumulation of significant levels of indebtedness. At the same time, the OED evaluation noted that, over time, the Bank internalized emerging lessons and shifted its emphasis accordingly. The study concluded with a number of findings and recommendations that cut across sectors and are broadly applicable for many regions: holding lending at prudent levels in a new country context, or after a long hiatus in lending, while building a knowledge base, with convincing evidence of government and societal ownership of the assistance program; promoting stakeholder inclusion and government ownership and leadership of aid coordination; improving the effectiveness of Bank instruments and defining clear strategies; carrying out relevant and timely economic and sector work (ESW); taking a comprehensive, long term approach to public sector management reform; according high priority to poverty monitoring and analysis of governance from the beginning of Bank involvement in a country; and ensuring transparency and accountability, including wide dissemination of Bank studies.

Management, in its Response to the OED study, welcomed the review and expressed its general agreement with the thrust of the evaluation. Management found the report's recommendations acceptable, with a few qualifications (see MR), and noted that it could have benefited from analysis that took more into account what was known about transition economies at the time critical support decisions were taken. Management sought the Committee's guidance on whether an assessment of a seminal event, such as the transition in Eastern Europe and the former Soviet Union, using perfect hindsight, was useful as a guide to action to teams that must take support decisions in real time in rapidly evolving crisis and near-crisis situations.

Conclusions and Next Steps. Members welcomed the OED evaluation and the Management Response and commended the staff for preparing an informative, well-written and candid assessment. They broadly agreed with the report's findings and recommendations, and noted that it had clearly articulated several important lessons from the unique transition experience in the ECA region. The Committee focused its discussion on the extent to which management has taken the OED recommendations on board and sought more details on how the response could be best implemented, especially in the areas of legal and judicial reform, privatization, financial sector, debt analysis, turnaround situations and poverty analysis. Interest was also reiterated in the efficacy of CAS triggers and other benchmarks. Some members wished that the report had also addressed a few additional areas, including: cooperation with the Fund; investment outcomes of the IFC; analysis of the differences across countries; focus on results and comparisons with other institutions; and decentralization. Among issues identified for going forward were: employment generation; lessons on current practices on governance and public sector management; portability of lessons across sectors and regions; capacity building and use of local expertise; aid coordination; and the issue of "gap countries".

Among the specific issues raised by the Committee were:

Lessons learned: utility of perfect hindsight approach.
Many members agreed with the management that the transition period in the ECA region was an unprecedented event, and many of the changes were difficult to foresee. However, they also emphasized the usefulness of the perfect hindsight approach employed by OED, given the Bank's frequent involvement in post-conflict and emergency situations, and noted that lessons deriving from a perfect hindsight approach are useful not only in checking assumptions, identifying blind spots and judging the validity of conventional wisdom, but also in assessing when and how corrective actions or adjustments to strategies could be undertaken. One member wanted to know more on variations in the pattern of Bank Group engagement in policy dialogue with clients across the region, given the volatile political situation in many countries, and

the impact on the Bank's portfolio. OED noted that the high fluctuation in policy dialogue in transition countries was partly due to the uneven level of civil society development across the region and the legacy of high reliance on the state. Management concurred with OED's view and added that frequent government changes in many cases could be perceived as a positive phenomenon for countries previously not accustomed to free elections. Management also underlined the positive impact of decentralization of the Bank in maintaining consistent dialogue with the clients. Members concurred with the OED recommendation to emphasize the implementation aspect, as opposed to legislative actions, and asked whether a new approach will be reflected in the triggers and benchmarks for the upcoming CASs. Management agreed with the necessity to shift the focus to actual implementation and noted that recent CASs, as well as APLs and other operations are increasingly putting more emphasis on outcomes.

Role of the Bank and results.
Speakers acknowledged the important role played by the Bank in the ECA region, and stressed the significance of the Bank's analytical work. Some members stressed the importance of looking at the overall results of Bank interventions (including IFC investments) and comparing them with other institutions, such as the EBRD. One member questioned whether the Bank possesses enough flexibility for quick and effective engagement in "turnaround" situations, given the rigidity of CPIA criteria. Management agreed that the CPIA is by definition a backward-oriented assessment tool, and not best suited as a basis for allocating resources in turnaround situation. Management also noted that there was continuous discussion within the institution to improve the CPIA methodology. In management's view, although IDA has overall been quite forthcoming in accommodating some incremental resource needs in turnaround situations; it would be equally important for bilateral donors to stay engaged and play a substantive and constructive role.

Sectoral focus and sequencing.
Members welcomed the report's recommendation to focus on gov-

ernance, reforms in judicial, legal and financial areas, as well as on the ex-ante analytical work on governance, and stressed the importance of wide-range capacity building to expedite the process. Management replied that the ECA Region is increasingly giving more prominence to the legal and judicial reform components in many of the programmatic loans, as well as to the freestanding legal and judicial reform operations. Management also noted that many aspects of legal and judicial reform agenda are financed through the IDF (Institutional Development Facility) grants. Several members noted that the paper would have benefited from additional coverage of such topics as employment, decentralization and co-operation with the Fund. OED replied that, although it was not a joint or parallel evaluation with the IMF, its analysis did take a careful look at the IMF programs in many of those countries, especially in the context of the Bank's adjustment lending. On employment, management noted that the Region has been advocating flexibility of the labor markets as part of the reform agenda, but there certainly was a gap in impact on unemployment. Management informed the members that the Region is currently finalizing a flagship regional report on employment, which will shed more light on that issue.

Privatization. While some members agreed with the management's view that in many cases rapid privatization was necessary to make the reform process irreversible, others noted the importance of adjusting reform sequencing to country circumstances and adopting a more gradual approach, e.g. choosing commercialization as a substitute to full privatization in the energy sector. OED noted that while it agrees with the critical importance of commercialization, especially in the energy sector, actual privatization is very much dependent on the country situation. Management replied that the new guidance to the staff does follow up on the OED, OEG and OEU recommendations to consider the full range of options—from pure public to private interventions—depending on country circumstances. Some members felt that the paper would have benefited from a more detailed cross-regional comparative analysis of privatization outcomes

and lessons learned in the process, impact on enterprise performance, employment, prices and their affordability, tax revenues, development of indigenous entrepreneurship, and poverty. Management noted that in many cases the reform agenda, and namely the quick privatization, had been advocated by the reformist governments themselves, which had often moved at a faster pace than the Bank. Management stressed that in some countries quick privatization, combined with the related FDI, has been instrumental in cementing a culture of market-orientation.

Debt sustainability. Some members supported the OED finding that the current high indebtedness of some CIS states was partly induced by the underestimated depth of the recession, but noted that resource flows were vital for future growth and that lending decisions were appropriate given all the analysis of debt capacity at that time. In that context, some members asked whether the debt systems have been improved and are currently in place to avoid this type of situation in future. OED replied that systems are being put in place, citing creation of the position of a Director for debt as one of the major steps in that direction. Management noted that economic growth throughout the region since 2000 has contributed to significant reduction of the share of debt service to exports (approximately 20 percent) in the most indebted CIS-7 countries, but, at the same time, acknowledged their persistent vulnerability in that regard. Management also added that in most of the countries in the region, debt is more of a collective, rather than just a Bank problem. Some members expressed their interest in the Bank's future approach in similar situations and the use of grant financing. One member called for more flexibility in the Bank's approach towards the "gap" countries—those that have higher than IDA threshold income levels, but lack creditworthiness of a typical IBRD country—at the upcoming IDA discussions. Management replied that it would actively continue to engage, including on the IDA front, to find solutions for the "gap" countries.

Poverty reduction. Members agreed with the management's view that the drastic drop in living standards in many transitional economies was hard to foresee, and emphasized the importance of continuous poverty monitoring. One member wished the report had contained information on income distribution and changes therein in the region. OED concurred with the members' view on the crucial importance of poverty monitoring, but noted that some countries in the region still lack the capacity to collect data. OED also noted that the report includes a table showing changes in income distribution in the region, and the text mentions the increases in inequality.

Cooperation. A member urged the Bank to stay engaged in the region and maintain close association with the EU initiatives, given the persistence of considerable differences in income levels inside the EU. Management noted that it is planning to continue cooperation with the EU and stressed that the EU accession of some countries provided a strong stimulus for the whole region.

Chander Mohan Vasudev, Chairman

Executive Summary

1. Management disagreed with the unsatisfactory rating for the early period in Russia. Recent OED project assessments show that the effectiveness of Bank assistance to Albania has improved since the CAE was written.

1. La Administración no estuvo de acuerdo en calificar de insatisfactorio el período inicial en Rusia. Según evaluaciones recientes de proyectos realizadas por el DEO, la eficacia de la asistencia prestada por el Banco a Albania ha mejorado desde que se redactó el informe de evaluación de la asistencia prestada a ese país.

1. La direction rejette la notation « insatisfaisant » pour la période initiale du programme d'aide en Russie. Les évaluations récentes de l'OED montrent que l'aide de la Banque à l'Albanie est plus efficace que lors de l'évaluation initiale.

Chapter 1

1. This report covers the transition countries of the Europe and Central Asia Region of the World Bank; it does not cover other transitional countries, such as China or Mongolia.

2. Serbia and Montenegro is not included, except where otherwise noted.

3. Throughout this report, references to the Bank or the World Bank should be understood to include the International Development Association (IDA), and references to loans to include credits.

4. There was no definitive statement of Bank objectives at the beginning of the transition; see, for example, World Bank (1996).

5. The 1996 WDR on the transition confirms this emphasis (World Bank 1996, pp. 70-71). More recently, client surveys in 9 countries (out of 12 carried out in transition countries) rate the Bank as having relatively low effectiveness in giving the appropriate priority to poverty reduction, or in reducing poverty; in

4 of the 9, however, the clients themselves did not assign great importance to poverty reduction.

6. Romania had also been an early member of the Bank, but relations were effectively broken off in the early 1980s. Yugoslavia was in the midst of political breakup at the start of the 1990s.

7. For example, OED's review of the Armenia Second Structural Adjustment TA Credit found that this project, which supported four adjustment operations and was the catalyst for significant resources from other donors, was the key to reform.

8. Poland in 1994; Russia and Kyrgyz Republic in 1995; Belarus, Estonia, Ukraine, and Azerbaijan in 1996-97.

9. Even in the agricultural sector, poverty monitoring and lessons learned about poverty impact in projects were rare (Heath 2003 pp. 17-18).

10. The Russia CAE noted (OED 2002c, p. 11) that "Until 2000, the government was not interested in Bank studies on the expenditure side of the budget or financial accountability." Some work may have been done in the context of non-sector-specific country economic memoranda.

11. This report deals only with the World Bank.

12. Svejnar (2002) provides data on a number of areas of performance not covered here, including inflation, exchange rates and current accounts, external debt, budgets and taxes, employment and wages, and several additional social indicators.

13. Conceptual and measurement problems make it difficult to compare pre- and post-transition GDP data; the likelihood that the former was overestimated and the latter underestimated means the collapse may not have been as deep as these data indicate. However, the decline in many countries was undoubtedly severe.

14. It is not clear to what extent the recent growth in CIS countries reflects recovery rather than new in-

vestment, or the degree to which it is influenced by the performance of the Russian economy.

15. The measures of inequality at the beginning of the period were skewed by shortages, administered pricing, and privileged access to some goods, so the deterioration is probably less than the numbers indicate.

16. For comparison, life expectancy in middle-income countries worldwide rose by 1.4 years, and in low- income countries by 1.9 years, during the same period.

17. Including Serbia and Montenegro.

18. Belarus, Turkmenistan, and Uzbekistan still rated a 1 or 2 in trade and foreign exchange liberalization.

19. Management disagreed with the unsatisfactory rating of the earlier period for Russia, noting that many reforms implemented after 1998 reflected Bank advice provided during 1992-98 and built on reforms of that period. Recent project evaluations by OED show that the effectiveness of Bank assistance to Albania has improved since the CAE was prepared in 1998. The satisfactory category includes moderately satisfactory ratings, and unsatisfactory includes moderately unsatisfactory.

20. Of CAEs for 40 non-transition countries, 29, or 73 percent, rated outcome for the most recent period satisfactory, compared to the two-thirds for transition countries. Taking all periods rated, 33 of 52 (63 percent) have satisfactory outcomes, compared to 55 percent for ECA. It should be noted that the country programs chosen for evaluation, both for ECA and Bankwide, were not a random sample, but rather a function of business needs and CAS schedules.

21. Client surveys show that the clients themselves often give little priority to such issues as improving governance, strengthening civic participation, and reflecting different viewpoints across the population.

22. The satisfactory category includes highly satisfactory, satisfactory, and moderately satisfactory. It is not unusual to find a "disconnect" between ratings at the project level and outcomes at the country level.

23. Sachs, Zinnes, and Eilat (2000) create seven clusters of countries based on similar initial conditions, but they do not provide additional explanatory power with respect to project outcomes; i.e., the range of outcome ratings within each of the seven clusters is large. For example, the proportion of satisfactory outcomes

ranges from 5 to 96 percent in the western FSU, and from 0 to 97 percent in Central Asia.

24. The low rate of satisfactory outcomes in terms of commitments for Russia reflects unsatisfactory ratings by OED of major adjustment loans. The ECA Region disagreed with those ratings.

25. Dedicated lending for some sectors, including PSD and PSM, is only a fraction of total lending for those sectors, much of which comes from economic policy operations, so the ratings may overstate their success.

26. The tasks rated in ECA included 4 in Turkey out of a total of 79. Ratings are not provided for individual countries.

Chapter 2

1. These papers were based on available OED and Regional evaluative material, as well as on other country, sector, and project material and interviews with Bank staff. See the Bibliography.

2. It was noted in Chapter 1 that PSD, institutions, and public accountability and governance were the areas most frequently identified by CAEs as needing greater attention.

3. In addition, many critical issues in transport are related to PSD.

4. During FY89-03, the Bank lent US$2.4 billion to transition countries for 35 PSD projects. About US$14 billion additional lending had PSD components, including the approximate share of these components only, PSD-related assistance amounted to roughly US$10.5 billion. The analysis in this section is based on 133 projects, of which 87 have been closed and rated, as well as on documents from OED and elsewhere.

5. World Bank (2002b) presents these themes in detail.

6. The results are not markedly different if only commitments with satisfactory outcomes are used. However, since many of the projects contained non-PSD components, the ratings may have little meaning.

7. PSD commitments per capita were plotted against the EBRD scores for enterprise reform (annex table A.7). The results suggest that an increase in the former of US$36 is associated with a full point increase in the EBRD index, the difference between the extent of reforms in Uzbekistan and in Latvia.

8. Several Background Papers for this evaluation touch on this debate. Kogut and Spicer (forthcoming)

review the literature on the Bank's role in the privatization process. See also Svejnar (2002) for a summary of the debate; the transition country CAEs for comments on the Bank's role in those countries; and the country papers (Bager 2002; Blaszczyk, Cukowski, and Siwiñska 2002; Jandosov 2002) for the point of view of some borrowers.

9. Nellis (2002) elucidates the states of mind that prevailed in selected countries and in the Bank, and describes the reforms as they evolved. He concludes that although in many cases privatization could have—and probably should have—been better managed, it has proven its worth in CEE countries, while the CIS countries that tried to transit without much change of ownership have not had much success.

10. Institutional components did appear in adjustment and rehabilitation loans before 1996 to the Czech Republic, Hungary, Moldova, Poland, and Romania.

11. The World Bank lends a degree of impartiality in facilitating enterprise reforms that investment banks do not. The signal sent to investors by IFC or the EBRD when they invest their own money is extremely valuable.

12. In recent evaluative work on Bosnia and Herzegovina, OED found that the Region continued to support mass privatization through vouchers beyond the mid-1990s, when a consensus had already emerged that this was a mistake.

13. The Region has acknowledged that in at least one case (Armenia), earlier and more aggressive attention to improvements in the business environment might have led more quickly to dynamic growth.

14. This section is based on a review of Bank assistance to 14 countries, selected to be representative of the different categories of countries: Russia (in a category of its own), one Baltic state (Latvia), three Central European countries (Hungary, Poland, and Romania), two in Eastern Europe (Moldova and Ukraine), two in South-Eastern Europe (Albania and Bulgaria), and five other CIS countries (Armenia, Georgia, Kazakhstan, Kyrgyz, and Tajikistan). This sample includes the largest country and the smallest, the richest and the poorest, and one of the most and one of the least democratic states.

15. http://www.worldbank.org/wbi/governance/govdata2002/. These data are associated with large margins of error and should be used with caution. Two points were not recorded for 1996. For the underlying methodology, see Kaufman, Kraay, and Mastruzzi (2003).

16. These reports, expected to be issued every three years, are based on the firm-level Business Environment and Enterprise Performance Surveys (BEEPS), carried out in collaboration with the EBRD.

17. Kogut and Spicer (forthcoming) conclude that economics has been the only real player in policy discussions, and that sociology and political science were neglected. ECA's publication *Transition: The First Ten Years* (World Bank 2002b) recognizes the primacy of political factors in determining economic developments.

18. OED's recent report on *Mainstreaming Anti-Corruption Activities in World Bank Assistance* (OED forthcoming) similarly called for a better understanding of social and political factors at the country level to enhance the quality and impact of Bank advice and improve the design of anti-corruption interventions.

19. Such a long-term approach may not be appropriate for all countries, such as those that have graduated or for which EU accession issues shorten the time horizon. Even in these cases, however, institution building should be placed within a long-term framework. The Region notes that it is already applying this lesson.

20. World Bank (2000a) and the World Bank/EBRD Business Environment and Enterprise Performance Surveys (1999 and 2002).

21. Jandosov (2002, p. 8) acknowledges the importance of Bank assistance in introducing transparent procurement procedures in Kazakhstan's public sector, only one of many examples.

22. OED's evaluation of knowledge sharing in the Bank found that while clients welcome improvements in the accessibility and timeliness of Bank information, they still see a need to improve dissemination of the Bank's knowledge at the country level (OED 2003, p. 27).

23. The Region notes that most adjustment operations in this sector now have measures to promote transparency, including publishing information such as audit reports, reporting to Parliament, and setting up Web sites.

24. The Region notes that in recent months the organization of this work has improved: projects are now jointly overseen by the Region and the Legal Department, and a thematic group has been created that includes all stakeholders.

25. This section is based on a review of 26 country programs, including policy papers, ESW, and almost 200 projects identified as having financial sector development objectives during the period 1991–00. OED is currently carrying out an evaluation of the Bank's financial sector assistance worldwide.

26. Informal financial sector work may have been prepared, but was not reviewed for this evaluation. The joint IMF–World Bank Financial Sector Assessment Program (FSAP), initiated in 1999, was also not reviewed; OED is undertaking a separate evaluation of the this program.

27. See, for example, Báger (2002, p. 5) on the Bank's role in Hungary, and Blaszczyk, Curkowski, and Siwińska (2002, p. 26) for a description of a highly satisfactory financial sector adjustment project linking bank recapitalization to enterprise restructuring in Poland.

28. The countries can be broken down into four groups, but the CIS countries are concentrated in the weak and partial reformer categories, while all of the CEB countries fall into the progressing and advanced reformer categories (see also annex table A.7).

29. The ECA Region and the Bank's Financial Sector Board are putting in place new procedures to ensure that financial sector staff review all such operations.

30. This section is based on a review of 83 sector reports and 60 projects with social protection components, of which two-thirds have been closed and rated. Some projects included components in several areas, so the sum of the numbers of projects referred to in this section is greater than 60.

31. All five of the CASs in 1992 raised this topic, as did about 60 percent of the CASs in the subsequent three years.

32. For example, Andrews and Ringold (1999); Fox (2002); Lindeman, Rutkowski, and Sluchynskyy (2000); World Bank (2000b). This evaluation confirms that if the report were rewritten today to reflect experience, most of the original recommendations would remain, although a few new ones might be added, and relative emphases changed.

33. This study was never adopted as official Bank policy in the pension area, but it became a reference for policymakers and Bank staff, and was perceived externally as the Bank's vision for pension reform.

34. Nine investment and two adjustment operations had employment service components. Nine pieces

of ESW focused on labor markets, unemployment, and employment services, but none preceded projects.

35. The Bank supported pension reform in 9 investment and 17 adjustment loans, in a total of 16 countries. The outcomes of most have been rated satisfactory, or, if still active, they are being implemented satisfactorily. In only two cases were reforms analyzed in advance of the policy debate, and in only one (Poland) was the reform adopted. Early failures included loans to Belarus, Romania, and Russia. OED's upcoming evaluation of pension reform Bankwide will assess in more detail the effectiveness of the Bank's direct assistance in the pension area.

36. For a Polish view of the Bank's contribution to pension reform, see Blaszczyk, Cukrowski, and Siwińska 2002, pp. 32–33.

37. Eleven investment and 18 adjustment loans had social assistance components, and 40 reports were written. With a few notable exceptions since 1998, the ESW focused mostly on documenting problems rather than on analyzing desirable policy reforms.

38. Only the effort in Romania was linked to a particular loan.

39. Lack of administrative, including analytical, capacity is cited as a major impediment to improving social assistance programs in the transition economies by the ECA Region (Andrews and Ringold 1999; World Bank 2000b).

40. The ECA review of its social protection activities reached a similar conclusion (World Bank, 2000b).

41. Some recent adjustment loans have begun to address labor market issues.

42. The success in Russia was temporary, as the government could not afford to maintain the real value of the minimum pension after the 1998 fiscal crisis.

43. A good *Regional* assessment of social protection strategy was issued in 2000 (World Bank 2000b).

44. A notable recent exception is the 2002 CAS for Bulgaria.

45. The findings in this section are based on 102 projects in 24 countries (there were no projects in Belarus or Turkmenistan) that were either dedicated energy projects or had an energy component, as well as on information from CAEs and other Bank documents.

46. As noted earlier, underlying the objectives of the Bank was the concern that reforms might be reversed if they were not implemented quickly and suc-

cessfully. The Georgia Sector Adjustment Credit was the only project to mention the explicit objective of combating corruption.

47. World Bank (1999). The scores are based on a questionnaire completed in 1998 by World Bank staff with experience in the energy sector in 115 countries, including the 24 ECA countries.

48. A point was awarded if either generation or distribution or both had experienced some privatization. ESMAP criteria do not cover financial performance, and in some cases (Georgia, for example, because of poor performance in governance and law and order), successful structural reforms did not lead to improved financial performance during the time period covered by this report.

49. These assessments do not correspond to OED ratings of the projects, but are based rather on an assessment of the outcome of the energy component only of each project, as revealed in evaluation reports. The other countries judged fair to good were the Czech Republic, Kazakhstan, and Moldova; they received scores of 4, 4, and 3 respectively on policy reform, and are in the middle range of improvement in energy efficiency.

50. Taking only the 31 projects classified as energy projects, 87 percent received satisfactory ratings for the Bank's performance, compared with 70 percent of all energy and mining projects Bankwide.

51. This conclusion affirms other OED findings, for example, in the evaluation of the Comprehensive Development Framework (CDF Secretariat 2003).

52. This conclusion is in line with Bank operational policy.

53. For example, in Bulgaria and Kazakhstan, the Bank needed to understand the business environment in which SOEs operated in order to impose hard budget constraints and financial discipline. Cutting them off from the budget and imposing penalties for a build-up of interenterprise arrears achieved little if they simply financed their losses from the state banking system.

54. Good examples were Bulgaria, Kazakhstan, the Kyrgyz Republic (despite limited energy lending), Lithuania, Poland, Romania, and the Russian Federation.

55. This is a key finding in OED, OEG, and OEU (2003a, p. 44), which also discusses individual country experience.

Chapter 3

1. OED's evaluation of knowledge sharing by the Bank (OED 2003) echoes this recommendation.

2. OED's *2001 Annual Review of Development Effectiveness* (OED 2002a, pp. 25, 59) confirmed the critical importance of ESW for country programs, and called for a strong evaluative framework to ensure its continued effectiveness. Activity completion summaries for ESW, while mandated for tasks above $50,000, are often not done.

3. Jandosov (2002, p. 15) stresses the importance of building local analytical and research capacity through joint ESW and the role of its dissemination in promoting dialogue and consensus in the country. OED's evaluation of knowledge sharing also finds that "clients give particular emphasis to enhanced efforts by the Bank to incorporate local knowledge and collaborate with local experts, strengthen institutional capacity, and expand in-country knowledge dissemination" (OED 2003, p. 29).

4. The Region points out that they have made country-by-country or subregional attempts to encourage this kind of behavior; and that a lot of donor coordination already takes place in the EU accession countries.

Annex C

1. In some cases, the positions listed are those held at the time of the interview; some of the people no longer occupy the same positions.

Annex D

1. This observation is not fully consistent with another of the report's observation: that capital market development was sometimes overemphasized in the early years of transition.

BIBLIOGRAPHY

***Background Papers for the evaluation can be identified by the asterisk (*) that precedes them. All papers will be available on the study Web site:
<http://www.worldbank.org/oed/transitioneconomies>.***

Andrews, Emily, and Dena Ringold. 1999. "Safety Nets in Transition Economies: Toward a Reform Strategy." Social Protection Discussion Paper No. 9914. World Bank, Europe and Central Asia Region, Human Development Sector Unit, Washington, D.C.

*Báger, Gusztáv. 2002. "Evaluation of the World Bank's Role in the Transition: Hungary." OED, Washington, D.C. <http://www.worldbank.org/oed/transitioneconomies>.

Barr, Nicholas (ed.). 1994. *Labor Markets and Social Policy in Central and Eastern Europe.* New York: Oxford University Press.

*Bates, Robin W. Forthcoming. "Evaluation of World Bank Assistance to the Transition Economies: Energy Sector Background Paper." OED, Washington, D.C. <http://www.worldbank.org/ oed/transitioneconomies>.

*Blaszczyk, Barbara, Jacek Cukrowski, and Joanna Siwiñska. 2002. "Evaluation of the World Bank's Role in the Transition: Poland." OED, Washington, D.C. <http://www.worldbank.org/oed/transitioneconomies>.

CDF Secretariat. 2003. *Toward Country-led Development: A Multi-partner Evaluation of the Comprehensive Development Framework.* Washington, D.C.: World Bank.

de Melo, Martha, Cevdet Denizer, Alan Gelb, and Stoyan Tenev. 2001. "Circumstances and Choice: The Role of Initial Conditions and Policies in Transition Economies." *The World Bank Economic Review* 15 (1): 1–31.

*Desai, Raj. Forthcoming. "Private Sector Development Assistance to the Transition Economies: A Decade of World Bank Lending." OED, Washington, D.C. <http://www.worldbank.org/oed/transitioneconomies>.

Djankov, Simeon, and Peter Murrell. 2000. *Determinants of Enterprise Restructuring in Transition: An Assessment of the Evidence.* Washington, D.C.: World Bank.

EBRD (European Bank for Reconstruction and Development). 2001. *Transition Report 2001: Energy in Transition.* London.

————. 1999. *Transition Report 1999: Ten Years of Transition.* London.

Falcetti, Elisabetta, Martin Raiser, and Peter Sanfey. 2002. "Defying the Odds: Initial Conditions, Reforms and Growth in the First Decade of Transition." *Journal of Comparative Economics* 30 (2): 229–50.

Fox, Louise. 2002. *Safety Nets in Transition Economies: A Primer Paper.* Social Protection Discussion Paper 306, World Bank Institute. Washington, D.C.: World Bank.

Grootaert, Christiaan, and Jeanine Braithwaite. 1998. "Poverty Correlates and Indicator-Based Targeting in Eastern Europe and the Former Soviet Union." Policy Research Working Paper 1943. Washington, D.C.: World Bank

Gupta, Poonam, Rachel Kleinfeld, and Gonzalo Salinas. 2002. "Legal and Judicial Reform in Europe and Central Asia." OED Working Paper, Washington, D.C.

Heath, John. 2003. "Agriculture Policy Reform in the ECA Transition Economies, 1991–2002: An Assessment of the World Bank's Approach." OED Working Paper, Washington, D.C.

*Jandosov, Oraz. 2002. "Evaluation of World Bank Assistance to Kazakhstan (Borrower's point of view)."

OED, Washington, D.C. <http://www.world bank.org/oed/transitioneconomies>.

Johnston, Timothy. 2002. "Supporting a Healthy Transition: Lessons from Early World Bank Experience in Eastern Europe." OED Working Paper, Washington, D.C.

Kaufmann, D., A. Kraay, and M. Mastruzzi. 2003. *Governance Matters III: Governance Indicators for 1996–2002.* World Bank Policy Research Working Paper, Washington, D.C.

*Kogut, Bruce, and Andrew Spicer. Forthcoming. "Critical and Alternative Perspectives on International Assistance to Post-Communist Countries: A Review and Analysis." OED, Washington, D.C. <http://www.worldbank.org/oed/transitioneconomies>.

Krishnaswamy, V., and Gary Stuggins. 2002. "Private Sector Participation in the Power Sector in ECA Countries: Lessons Learnt from the Last Decade." World Bank Working Paper, Europe and Central Asia Region, Infrastructure and Energy Department, Washington, D.C.

*Landell-Mills, Pierre. Forthcoming. "An Evaluation of World Bank Assistance for Governance, Public Sector Management and Institution Building in the Transition Economies 1990–2002." OED, Washington, D.C. <http://www.worldbank.org/oed/transitioneconomies>.

*Levy, Fred. Forthcoming. "World Bank Assistance for Financial Sector Development in the ECA Transition Economies." OED, Washington, D.C. <http://www.worldbank.org/oed/transitioneconomies>.

Lindeman, David, Michal Rutkowski, and Oleksiy Sluchynskyy. 2000. *The Evolution of Pension Systems in Eastern Europe and Central Asia: Opportunities, Constraints, Dilemmas and Emerging Practices.* Washington, D.C.: World Bank.

Lovei, Laszlo. 1998. "Energy in Europe and Central Asia, a Sector Strategy for the World Bank." Discussion Paper No. 393. Washington, D.C.: World Bank.

*Nellis, John. 2002. "The World Bank, Privatization and Enterprise Reform in Transition Economies: a Retrospective Analysis." OED Working Paper, Washington, D.C. <http://www.worldbank.org/oed/transitioneconomies>.

OED (Operations Evaluation Department). Forthcoming. *Mainstreaming Anti-Corruption Activities in World Bank Assistance: A Review of Progress Since 1997.* Operations Evaluation Department. Washington, D.C.: The World Bank.

———. 2003. *Sharing Knowledge: Innovations and Remaining Challenges.* Catherine Gwin, task manager. OED Study Series. Washington, D.C.: World Bank.

———. 2002a. *2001 Annual Review of Development Effectiveness: Making Choices.* Bill Battaile, task manager. OED Study Series. Washington, D.C.: The World Bank.

———. 2002b. "Evaluation of World Bank Assistance to the Transition Economies: Entry Workshop." May 15. Transcript. Operations Evaluation Department, Washington, D.C.

———. 2002c. *Assisting Russia's Transition: An Unprecedented Challenge.* OED Study Series. Gianni Zanini, task manager. Washington, D.C.: World Bank.

———. 2001. *The Drive to Partnership: Aid Coordination and the World Bank.* OED Study Series. John Eriksson, task manager. Washington, D.C.: World Bank

OED, OEG, and OEU, World Bank Group. 2003a. *Power for Development: A Review of the World Bank Group's Experience with Private Participation in the Electricity Sector.* Rafael Dominguez, Fernando Manibog, and Stephan Wegner, task managers. OED Study Series. Washington, D.C.: World Bank.

———. 2003b. *Extractive Industries and Sustainable Development: An Evaluation of World Bank Group Experience.* Vols. 1–4. OED Study Series. Washington, D.C.: World Bank.

Sachs, Jeffrey, Clifford Zinnes, and Yair Eilat. 2000. "Patterns and Determinants of Economic Reform in Transition Economies: 1990–98." Harvard Institute for International Development, Consulting Assistance on Economic Reform II Discussion Paper No. 61. Cambridge, MA.

Sahgal, Vinod, and Deepa Chakrapani. 2000. "Clean Government and Public Financial Accountability," OED Working Paper No. 17, Washington, D.C.

Shihata, Ibrahim. 1991. *The World Bank in a Changing World: Selected Essays*. Dordrecht: Nijhoff (Kluwer Academic).

*Svejnar, Jan. 2002. "Assistance to the Transition Economies: Were There Alternatives?" OED Working Paper, Washington, D.C. <http://www.worldbank.org/oed/transitioneconomies>.

*Thompson, Lawrence. Forthcoming. "Social Protection and the Transition." OED, Washington, D.C. <http://www.worldbank.org/oed/transitioneconomies>.

World Bank. Forthcoming. *Power's Promise: Electricity Reforms in Eastern Europe and Central Asia*. World Bank Technical Paper. Washington, D.C.

———. 2004. *Anticorruption in Transition: Corruption in Enterprise-State Interactions in Europe and Central Asia, 1999-02*. Washington, D.C.

———. 2003. *Hidden Challenges to Education Systems in Transition Economies: Education Sector Strategy Paper for Europe and Central Asia Region*. Washington, D.C.

———. 2002a. "Economic Development and Private Sector Growth in the Low-income CIS Countries: Challenges and Policy Implications," CIS-7 Initiative Paper, ECSPF, Lucerne Conference of the CIS-7 Initiative, January 20-22, 2003.

———. 2002b. *Transition: The First Ten Years*. Washington, D.C.

———. 2001. "Training Program on Social Policy Reform in Transition Economies (SPRITE)." WBI Evaluation Briefs. Evaluation Unit, World Bank Institute, Washington, D.C.

———. 2000a. *Anticorruption in Transition— A Contribution to the Policy Debate*. Washington, D.C.

———. 2000b. *Balancing Protection and Opportunity. A Strategy for Social Protection in Transition Economies*. Washington, D.C.

———. 2000c. *Making Transition Work for Everyone: Poverty and Inequality in Europe and Central Asia*. Washington, D.C.

———. 2000d. *Reforming Public Sector Institutions and Strengthening Governance*. Washington, D.C.

———. 1999. "Global Energy Sector Reform in Developing Countries: A Scorecard." ESMAP (Energy Sector Management Assistance Program) Paper ESM219. Washington, D.C.

———. 1998. "Profile of Energy Sector Activities of the World Bank in Europe and Central Asia Region," Vol. I, "The Overall Profile." Working Paper 18891, Washington, D.C.

———. 1997a. "Central and Eastern Europe: Power Sector Reform in Selected Countries." ESMAP (Energy Sector Management Assistance Program) Report No. 196/97. July.

———. 1997b. *World Development Report: The State in a Changing World*. New York: Oxford University Press for the World Bank.

———. 1996. *World Development Report: From Plan to Market*. New York: Oxford University Press for the World Bank.

———. 1994. *Averting the Old-Age Crisis: Policies to Protect the Old and Promote Growth*. New York : Oxford University Press.

———. 1993. *The World Bank's Role in the Electric Power Sector: Policies for Effective Institutional, Regulatory and Financial Reform—A World Bank Policy Paper*. Washington, D.C.

———. 1992. *Governance and Development*. Washington, D.C.

———. 1983. *World Development Report: Management in Development*. New York: Oxford University Press for the World Bank.